She Defies

Powerful
Stories of Overcoming

HANNA OLIVAS
ALONG WITH 21 INSPIRING AUTHORS

© 2025 ALL RIGHTS RESERVED.

Published by She Rises Studios Publishing **www.SheRisesStudios.com.**

No part of this book may be reproduced or transmitted in any form whatsoever, electronic, or mechanical, including photocopying, recording, or by any informational storage or retrieval system without the expressed written, dated and signed permission from the publisher and co-authors.

LIMITS OF LIABILITY/DISCLAIMER OF WARRANTY:

The co-authors and publisher of this book have used their best efforts in preparing this material. While every attempt has been made to verify the information provided in this book, neither the co-authors nor the publisher assumes any responsibility for any errors, omissions, or inaccuracies.

The co-authors and publisher make no representation or warranties with respect to the accuracy, applicability, or completeness of the contents of this book. They disclaim any warranties (expressed or implied), merchantability, or for any purpose. The co-authors and publisher shall in no event be held liable for any loss or other damages, including but not limited to special, incidental, consequential, or other damages.

ISBN: 978-1-966798-04-0

TABLE OF CONTENTS

INTRODUCTION 5

She Defies Against the Odds: A Testament to Resilience and Warrior Spirit
   By Hanna Olivas 7

A Beacon of Light: Defying Emotional Darkness
   By Anne-Marie Springer 14

Happiness Is in the Details
   By Jennifer Andrews, BSW, RSW 24

Kaleidoscope
   By Natalie Horseman 33

The Cyclops & the Amazon
   By Shannon Pereira 44

The Healing Rose
   By Nicole Lite 61

Be the Hero of Your Story
   By Hannah Darby, GMBPsP, SMACCPH 71

For Women Like Me
   By Tomia Minnis 80

Making a Message Out of a Mess
   By Emily Whitacre 91

Scars of Grace
   By Maureen Denise 101

The Day That Changed Forever
   By Jackie Otto 109

When My American Dream Died, I Rose from the Ashes
By Heather D. Mahoney 118

Teen Mom
By Stephanie Owens..128

Overcoming and Healing
By Suzanne E. Minshew...138

Living Takes Courage
By Ariel Balfour..147

The Trauma Freight Train
By Emily Cleghorn 156

The Tricks of Trauma Bonding
By Elizabeth Reece 164

A Journey of Resilience
By Angela Leapua...175

From Disastrously Burnt Out to Loving Life
By Jane Bromley 185

The Art of Learning to Trust and Believe in My Self
By Kerrie D. Stone..198

Defying the Darkness: A Journey from Despair to Empowerment
By Kimberly Laverdure 210

Dance With Your Demons
By Michele Benevento..221

INTRODUCTION

Welcome to *She Defies: Powerful Stories of Overcoming*, a collection of fierce, unforgettable journeys told by women who have triumphed over adversity. These 30 stories are more than just tales of survival; they are testaments to the strength and resilience that lie within each woman, waiting to be unleashed.

As you turn these pages, you'll step into the lives of women who've faced the unimaginable—barriers that range from personal loss and societal limitations to self-doubt and external struggles. But in each story, you'll also discover how these women defied the odds, rising above their circumstances with determination, courage, and grace. These aren't the stories of some distant, unrelatable figure; these are stories of women just like you. You'll find yourself nodding in recognition, feeling the raw emotion, and celebrating their victories as if they were your own.

You'll meet the woman who fought to make her voice heard in a male-dominated world. You'll journey with the single mother who, against all odds, raises her children with love and strength. And through every page, you'll realize one powerful truth: the struggles, the heartaches, and the moments of pure joy are what define us, what shape our stories—and what allow us to shine in a world that often tries to dim our light.

This book is an invitation to connect, to relate, and to be inspired. These are the stories of real women, with real experiences, defying the limitations set before them. And in doing so, they remind us all that we have the power to defy, too.

So, dive in. Feel the courage, the hope, and the undeniable strength that emanates from each page. This is your reminder that, no matter what life throws your way, you can rise, you can overcome, and you can defy.

Hanna Olivas

Founder and CEO of SHE RISES STUDIOS

https://www.linkedin.com/company/she-rises-studios/
https://www.facebook.com/sherisesstudios
https://www.instagram.com/sherisesstudios_llc/
www.SheRisesStudios.com

Author, Speaker, and Founder. Hanna was born and raised in Las Vegas, Nevada, and has paved her way to becoming one of the most influential women of 2022. Hanna is the co-founder of She Rises Studios and the founder of the Brave & Beautiful Blood Cancer Foundation. Her journey started in 2017 when she was first diagnosed with Multiple Myeloma, an incurable blood cancer. Now more than ever, her focus is to empower other women to become leaders because The Future is Female. She is currently traveling and speaking publicly to women to educate them on entrepreneurship, leadership, and owning the female power within.

She Defies Against the Odds:
A Testament to Resilience and Warrior Spirit

By Hanna Olivas

In a world where challenges often feel insurmountable, there exists a powerful archetype that stands tall, a beacon of strength and determination: the woman who defies against the odds. She embodies resilience, persevering through adversity with a spirit that cannot be broken. This chapter is a celebration of her journey—one that reflects the heart, mind, body, and soul intertwined with spirituality. It is a tribute to the unyielding strength that resides within every woman who chooses to show up, confront challenges, and rise above.

The Essence of Defiance

To defy means to resist or oppose boldly. It is an act of standing firm in the face of adversity, declaring that circumstances do not dictate one's fate. A woman who defies against the odds recognizes that challenges are not merely obstacles but opportunities for growth, transformation, and empowerment.

In the words of Maya Angelou, "I can be changed by what happens to me. But I refuse to be reduced by it." This profound statement captures the essence of defiance. It reminds us that while life may shape our experiences, it cannot define who we are. The journey of defiance is a choice—a conscious decision to rise above hardships, to embrace one's strength, and to forge a path that aligns with one's true self.

Heart: The Core of Resilience

At the heart of every woman who defies against the odds is an unwavering belief in herself and her worth. This inner strength fuels her resilience, allowing her to weather life's storms with grace and courage.

When faced with adversity, she draws upon the love and support of those around her, transforming her heartache into a source of power.

"Strength doesn't come from what you can do. It comes from overcoming the things you once thought you couldn't," said Rikki Rogers. This powerful quote emphasizes that true strength is not found in the absence of struggle but in the ability to confront and conquer it. It is through the heart that she discovers her capacity for love, empathy, and compassion—qualities that not only uplift her but also inspire others.

Her heart beats with the rhythm of hope, resonating with the belief that brighter days lie ahead. Even in the darkest moments, she remains steadfast, knowing that each challenge is a stepping stone toward a more profound understanding of herself and her purpose.

Mind: The Power of Perseverance

A resilient woman understands the significance of a strong mind. She cultivates a mindset that embraces challenges, viewing them as opportunities for learning and growth. When faced with setbacks, she refuses to be defeated; instead, she rises to the occasion, armed with determination and grit.

"Perseverance is not a long race; it is many short races one after the other," said Walter Elliot. This insightful perspective highlights that perseverance is not solely about endurance but also about the commitment to keep moving forward, step by step. Each small victory builds momentum, propelling her toward her ultimate goals.

Her mind becomes a sanctuary of positive thoughts, nurturing beliefs that empower her to keep going, even when the odds seem stacked against her. She practices self-care, engaging in mindfulness and reflection to cultivate mental clarity and emotional stability. Through this intentional practice, she learns to silence the inner critic and replace self-doubt with self-affirmation.

In moments of uncertainty, she repeats mantras that resonate with her spirit, such as "I am enough," "I am worthy," and "I will rise." These affirmations serve as reminders of her inherent strength, reinforcing her belief that she is capable of overcoming any obstacle in her path.

Body: The Vessel of Strength

A woman who defies against the odds embodies physical strength and vitality. She recognizes that her body is a vessel that carries her through life's challenges, and she honors it with care and respect. Engaging in physical activities, nourishing her body with healthy foods, and prioritizing rest are essential components of her journey.

"Take care of your body. It's the only place you have to live," said Jim Rohn. This powerful reminder emphasizes the importance of nurturing one's physical well-being. A strong body supports a resilient spirit, allowing her to face life's demands with confidence and energy.

Her body becomes a testament to her journey—a reflection of her battles fought and won. Each scar tells a story of resilience, and every drop of sweat signifies the effort she has invested in her personal growth. She embraces her imperfections, understanding that they are part of her unique narrative.

Soul: The Spiritual Connection

At the core of every woman who defies against the odds is a profound connection to her soul. This spiritual essence provides her with a sense of purpose and direction, guiding her through the ups and downs of life. She embraces her spirituality, drawing strength from her beliefs and values.

"Your soul knows the way. Trust it," said Jennifer Williamson. This powerful quote encapsulates the importance of trusting one's inner wisdom. A woman who defies understands that her intuition is a guiding force, leading her to make choices that align with her true self.

In times of uncertainty, she turns inward, seeking solace in prayer, meditation, or reflection. These practices nourish her soul and allow her to connect with a higher power. She understands that she is part of something greater than herself—a vast universe filled with possibilities and opportunities.

The Journey of Defiance

The journey of defiance is not linear; it is a winding path filled with twists and turns. There will be moments of triumph and moments of despair. What defines her is not the absence of struggle but her unwavering commitment to show up and keep going.

In her journey, she may face various challenges—personal, professional, or relational. Each hurdle presents an opportunity for growth, teaching her valuable lessons about resilience, perseverance, and the power of love. She learns that setbacks do not define her worth; instead, they shape her character and strengthen her resolve.

Through her experiences, she discovers the beauty of vulnerability. She allows herself to feel, to grieve, and to heal. In doing so, she cultivates compassion for herself and others, recognizing that everyone faces their own battles.

The Power of Community

A woman who defies against the odds often understands the importance of community. She surrounds herself with individuals who uplift and support her—a tribe of like-minded souls who share in her journey. This community becomes a source of strength, encouragement, and inspiration.

"Alone, we can do so little; together, we can do so much," said Helen Keller. This powerful reminder emphasizes the value of collaboration and connection. When women come together, they create an unbreakable bond that empowers each other to rise above challenges.

In moments of doubt, she turns to her community for support. They celebrate her victories, offer guidance in times of need, and remind her of her inherent strength. Together, they create a safe space where vulnerability is embraced, and growth is celebrated.

Authenticity: The Power of Being Real

At the core of her defiance is a commitment to authenticity. She chooses to show up as her true self, unafraid to embrace her flaws and imperfections. In a world that often pressures individuals to conform, she stands firm in her uniqueness.

"Be yourself; everyone else is already taken," said Oscar Wilde. This powerful reminder encourages individuals to embrace their individuality and authenticity. A woman who defies understands that her uniqueness is her superpower, allowing her to shine brightly in a world that may attempt to dim her light.

She speaks her truth, shares her story, and inspires others to do the same. In her authenticity, she cultivates connections that are genuine and deep. She attracts those who resonate with her spirit, creating relationships built on trust and understanding.

The Ripple Effect of Defiance

A woman who defies against the odds creates a ripple effect that extends far beyond her own life. Her resilience and strength inspire others to confront their challenges and embrace their own journeys. When she shows up, she encourages those around her to rise, creating a community of warriors who support and uplift one another.

"Your life is your story, and the adventure ahead of you is the journey to fulfill your own purpose and potential," said Kerry Washington. This powerful statement encapsulates the idea that each woman's journey is unique, and by embracing her path, she empowers others to do the same.

The stories of defiance and resilience become sources of inspiration, demonstrating that it is possible to rise above challenges and thrive. She becomes a role model for future generations, showing them that they, too, can defy the odds and create their own narratives of strength and empowerment.

Conclusion: Embracing the Warrior Within

As we conclude this chapter, let us remember the profound journey of the woman who defies against the odds. She embodies resilience, perseverance, and an unwavering spirit that cannot be broken. Through her heart, mind, body, and soul, she embraces the challenges that life presents, transforming them into opportunities for growth and empowerment.

In her journey, she learns that defiance is not merely an act of rebellion; it is a declaration of self-worth, a commitment to authenticity, and a celebration of community. She understands that her story is not just her own; it is a tapestry woven with the threads of countless women who have come before her and those who will follow.

As you embark on your own journey, remember the warrior within you. Embrace your challenges, trust in your strength, and know that you are not alone. Together, we can create a world where women rise above the odds, empowering one another to live authentically and fiercely.

In the words of Audre Lorde, "I am not free while any woman is unfree, even when her shackles are very different from my own." Let this reminder inspire us to stand together in solidarity, defying against the odds and creating a legacy of strength, resilience, and love for generations to come.

Anne-Marie Springer

Owner of The Wise Moose LLC

www.linkedin.com/in/anne-marie-springer-52958143
https://www.facebook.com/annemarie.springer.98A
https://www.instagram.com/annemarie.springer.98
https://wisemoosegrinds.com
https://MaryKay/ASpringer729

Anne-Marie Springer has had a passion for nursing and caring for others since she was young. Her passion led her to join the United States Navy and obtain her Nursing Degree from the University of South Florida. She worked in various nursing units, including Mother Baby, Emergency Room, and Family Practice. She retired from the Navy in 2009 and became a Population Health Nurse in Family Practice, serving the veteran population. Now retired after 25 years in nursing, Anne-Marie spends her time writing and working on her online business, Wise Moose Grinds. Her first book, "Help My Baby Won't Stop Crying!" was inspired by her experiences as a nurse and a mother and was published in 2023. Additionally, she contributed to the anthology "Becoming an Unstoppable Woman Entrepreneur Part II." Anne-Marie is a proud mother of three adult children and resides in Ohio with her husband and two lovable dogs.

A Beacon of Light: Defying Emotional Darkness

By Anne-Marie Springer

My mother ripped my doll out of my hand and, with a deafening scream, flung it at the kitchen window, breaking it with a resounding crack. At 5 years old, this was one of my first memories of her. Looking back on my childhood, the emotional darkness surrounding me felt like an overflow of negative energy from my parents, who, throughout their lives, appeared unable to embrace the light that comes from love, hope, and faith. I grew up believing that it was normal for mothers to scream, hit, and resent their children and for fathers to be missing in action. When my Father was home, he often dealt with my Mother's emotional outbursts by telling her to "go take a valium."

I know that my parents loved us, and there were occasions throughout the years when light pierced through the darkness of their misery, and they stopped quarreling for short periods. I remember happy picnics, trips to the amusement park, and holiday celebrations, but they struggled to embrace the clean and sparkling emotions that such activities bring to most of us. Connecticut was a beautiful place to be a child. Depending on the season, I was always happiest outside: underneath the trees, playing in the stream, laying on a blanket in the grass, or sledding down a snow-covered hill. I wish that my parents had experienced those feelings with me.

My father lived with us throughout junior high school but was absent physically, mentally, and emotionally. He remained lost in his pursuits and spent very little time and money taking care of his family and a lot on his hobbies, gambling, and chasing his dreams of wealth. As a result, my mother was overwhelmed with managing her household responsibilities, raising her children, and addressing her personal needs.

She was plagued by chronic stress and exhaustion, which led to resentment, emotional distress, reliance on prescription drugs, and an abusive dynamic in our home. It was not uncommon for my mother to scream, slam doors, and strike at us with whatever was within reach: a wooden spoon, ruler, or hairbrush. Sometimes, we would be disciplined for "general principles" because she just knew we had done "something wrong."

My mother struggled with balancing her numerous roles without support from my father. One night, she had enough of feeling neglected and having her needs unmet. She momentarily found a sense of empowerment, and when my Father was away, she packed our meager belongings into the trunk of her old, beat-up car, loaded my brother, sister, and me into it, and drove to Florida. We arrived at my uncle's home without warning to stay with his family. Despite not being close to my mother, my uncle and his family took us in with open arms.

They shared their home, food, spirituality, and guiding lights. My aunt and uncle taught me that violence is never acceptable, that abuse is not normal, and that there is always a way out of the darkness with hope and faith. These people shared their light and love with the world without asking for anything in return. Their guidance gave me the foundation to move forward and become the person I was meant to be rather than slipping back into self-pity and hopelessness.

My uncle helped my mother apply for and get accepted for government housing, and we moved into a unit in Tampa, Florida. In those days, public housing was referred to as the projects, and ours was a haven for prostitutes, poverty, illicit drugs, and deprivation, and I struggled not to be sucked into that destiny. The poverty mindset characterized by a fear of spending money, a constant search for the cheapest options, and the belief that wealth is out of reach was rampant in this community. My mother and father both displayed characteristics of this mindset, such as comparing themselves to others, expressing jealousy for those in better circumstances, describing themselves as victims, and overvaluing material things.

This mindset led my parents to make poor decisions with money. They failed to save or invest for their futures, and they remained unhappy and in poverty for the remainder of their lives. Searching for people who inspire and teach you to reach your highest potential is essential. I was blessed to have several high school teachers and counselors who taught me to focus on my strengths, set goals, practice gratitude, and reflect on all the positives in my life. This helped to rewire my brain to follow opportunities rather than dwell on limitations.

Once we were settled into housing, my mother filed for a divorce from my father and met a man at her job as a cocktail waitress. He was not a good man. She began staying out all night and leaving me at home to care for my brother and sister by myself. Once the divorce from my father was final, she married him while he was still in jail for abusing his children. He assured her that he was "framed."

He was released after pleading no contest and moved into our home, and verbal abuse became the norm. He had a disturbing habit of leering at me and would often stand outside the bathroom door while I was showering. He would ask me how he could improve his sexual performance with my mother and once went so far as to ask me to give him naked pictures of myself and my friends in return for 15 dollars. Darkness manifests in many forms.

My stepfather found my little brother, who was six at the time, to be an easy target for his tirades. He terrified him with screaming, verbal threats, and rough handling, and once, he went so far as to kick my brother in the ribs. After that event, Protective Services removed my brother from our home and sent him to live with my father. My sister withdrew into herself and stayed out of the way as much as possible.

My mother continued to withdraw due to her mental health issues and chose to ignore everything that my stepfather was doing; she was trapped in a mire of misery and despair. The last time my mother hit me, I was 16. She accused me of taking the mind-altering drugs that were so prevalent in our neighborhood, choosing to ignore facts that I was ranked 67 out of 610 in my class, in multiple honor societies, playing soccer and tennis, working at Mcdonald's, and taking care of my brother and sister. I ran away to a neighbor's house with only what I could hold in my arms. My stepfather chased me, swearing obscenities and saying that he would kill my first child. The neighbor called the police, and I was placed with my father in a small apartment that he shared with two women. My only regret was having to leave my sister behind, as her struggle with darkness would continue well into adulthood.

Throughout this turmoil and shades of darkness, I dreamed of leaving poverty behind and becoming a doctor. During these years, I discovered my inner strength and confidence with the support and encouragement of my teachers and coaches. I worked hard to become my best self and excelled in academics and athletics. I found solace in my studies, soccer, tennis, and various school clubs, and these became symbols of my growing inner strength and confidence amidst the chaos of my home life. My teachers, coaches, and counselors gave me positive role models and encouraged me to attend college.

I was determined to continue my education after high school, even though outside of school, I was surrounded by naysayers and people who told me it would be impossible to be anything other than a girl from the projects. I got a hand up when my uncle helped me obtain acceptance and a scholarship to a college in Maryland, and just like that, the curtain of darkness was drawn away.

When you struggle to overcome adversity, consider the quote attributed to motivational speaker Jim Rohn: "You are the average of the five people you spend the most time with." This suggests that the people we spend the most time with significantly influence how we think, behave, and interact with the world. Choose to surround yourself with those at the top of the field you want to pursue rather than those who moan, complain, and blame others for their situation.

I graduated high school and headed to college in Maryland to study Pre-Med with great pride and enthusiasm. My college campus was a world away from the projects. Located on a mountain, the air was always fresh, filled with the scent of fresh-cut grass, blooming flowers, and the chatter of other students brimming with ambition. I threw myself into my studies; my days were a blur of biology labs and late-night study sessions with newly made friends. I was well on my way to fulfilling my dream, but fate had other plans for me, and during my first semester, I discovered I was pregnant.

Although I had a steady boyfriend then, we did not intend to marry and have children until after we both got our college degrees. He did not want any part of helping me take care of our baby, as it would interfere with his plans and delay finishing his degree in Florida, and that ended our relationship. The news hit me like a sledgehammer, shattering my dreams of becoming a doctor. I felt a crushing weight of disappointment from myself, my uncle, and my teachers, who had placed so much faith in me.

With a heavy heart, I made the difficult decision to leave college and move in with my grandparents in Connecticut until I could make new plans for my growing family, my scholarship lost to the shifting sands of time. Devastatingly, I was not able to carry the baby to term, and the months that followed were a tumultuous storm of emotions. I felt adrift in a sea of doubt, guilt, and fear and unsure how to navigate my new reality. But in quiet moments, when my pain seemed almost unbearable, I was blessed with the gentle guidance of my grandmother and grandfather, urging me to keep pursuing my dreams. With their unwavering support, I found the strength to stand tall again.

I returned to Florida, stayed with friends, got a job, enrolled at the University of South Florida (USF), and started over. Tragedy struck again when my grandmother became gravely ill. I left college in the middle of a semester and went to Connecticut to help care for her. Struggling with what to do after my grandmother died and lacking enough funds to continue classes, I decided to join the Navy to establish some stability and purpose and return to college with the GI Bill. I knew this was a chance to redefine my destiny and take control of my life's narrative. Boot camp was demanding, but I found security in the discipline and structure and discovered a new reservoir of strength. After graduation, I moved on to a technical school in Memphis, where I met the love of my life, a marine attending the same military school.

We were married in a beautiful ceremony in his hometown, surrounded by friends and family within a few months of meeting so that we could be stationed together. My college plans were put on hold, and we moved to our first duty stations in California. Soon after, we welcomed our first baby, an adorable little boy who looked just like his father and was the light of our lives. Our life was filled with happiness and contentment, but darkness found me once again when our first son was tragically taken from us when he was 4 months old from Sudden Infant Death Syndrome (SIDS). SIDS is the unexplained death of a baby, usually less than a year old, that seems otherwise healthy. The cause of SIDS is still unknown but is believed to be caused by a malfunction in the part of the baby's brain that controls breathing and waking up from sleep.

My husband and I experienced a range of emotions that included anger, sadness, guilt, and shock, and sometimes, the pain still hits us after all these years, but we received a lot of support from our chaplain, family, and friends. If you experience the loss of a baby, please know that there are several organizations set up to help you, including First Candle, Children's Bereavement Center, March of Dimes, and Postpartum Support International. I continued to serve in the Navy, and we were ultimately blessed with three more beautiful rainbow babies. The name "rainbow baby" comes from the idea of a rainbow appearing in the sky after a storm or a dark and turbulent event.

Time flew by in a whirlwind of diapers, school days, exams, and military duties. I watched my children flourish and reach their full potential, and my heart swelled with love and pride. We made many happy memories traveling, visiting family, celebrating holidays and achievements, and being there for each other. But I knew I wasn't done yet, and my dreams of helping others on a grander scale remained. The years I spent in military service honed my discipline and focus, and I approached my studies with the same tenacity I had shown getting out of the projects. My textbooks became my tools for making a better life for myself and my family. My days were a careful balancing act of caring for my children, husband, patients, and studies, while my nights were a symphony of late-night feedings and cramming for exams. My husband took on more parental responsibilities, and his devotion to me and our children provided a beacon that guided me through my darkest hours.

I completed my nursing degree with the help of my husband, children, and the GI Bill, and my graduation from nursing school was a victory for me and my entire family. The proud smiles from my husband, children, and family brought tears to my eyes as I accepted my degree. I had defied the darkness of my past and forged a new identity for myself—I was Anne-Marie, the wife, the mother, the nurse, the survivor, and the warrior.

Upon graduation, I returned to the Navy as a commissioned Nurse Corps officer, and the moment I pinned the bars of a commissioned officer on my uniform, I felt a surge of pride that washed away the last vestiges of darkness from the difficulties in my past. My crisp white uniform reminded me of my chosen path, allowing me to serve my Country and community. The long hours spent in the wards and on deployment were hard on my family and me, and I missed out on time to cherish my husband's and children's milestones. Yet I persevered. My love for my family and country was a driving force that propelled me through the long, lonely nights and days in the hospital wards.

After 25 years of service, I retired from the Navy to spend more time with my husband and family and plant some roots in a community without worrying about imminent deployments. I spent the next 15 years caring for veterans as a Nurse at the Federal Health Care Center in North Chicago. I am now retired from nursing, and with my entrepreneurial spark ignited, I dreamed of creating something that would allow me to share my love of wellness and health beyond the confines of the hospital. My first book, *Help; My Baby Won't Stop Crying*, was published, followed by an anthology, *Becoming an Unstoppable Woman Entrepreneur Part II*. Additionally, I launched an online coffee business called Wise Moose Grinds in honor of my love of moose and good coffee.

After many trials and tribulations, I can proudly say that I am a retired Naval officer, retired nurse, published author, and owner of an online business. My days now are blended into a beautiful tapestry of family, business, and personal growth. The journey to overcoming adversity and defying the darkness can be long, painful, and treacherous. Still, you have the light and power within you to harness your resilience and be all you have dreamed of being.

My children have grown into successful adults, and my heart swells with pride when I see them pursuing their passions and following their dreams. My family has grown, and now my grandchild is the living embodiment of the hope I fought to keep alive. My husband remains my steadfast supporter, and I have built my world with him as my foundation.

As I look back on the long road I traveled, I know I have survived the darkness of my past and used it to reach my dreams. My life is a testament to the power of resilience, a story of a girl from the projects who had dared to dream and, in doing so, changed the trajectory of her and her family's destiny. I overcame adversity and turned it into my greatest asset by becoming a leader, a wife, a mother, and an entrepreneur.

May the legacy I built shine brightly for my children and generations to come.

As I sat in my home writing this, surrounded by peace and the love of my family, the warmth of my success, and the pride of a life devoted to service, I know that I have not just defied the darkness but transformed it into a beacon of light for others to follow. I hope my story of resilience and determination reminds you that no matter how bleak the present may feel to you, the future holds the promise of a brighter tomorrow. With hard work, unwavering faith, and the love of those who believe in you, you can achieve what others say is impossible. Onward, ho, let this be your first step out of the darkness; your journey has just begun!

Jennifer Andrews, BSW, RSW

Somiro Wellness
Life Coach | Therapist

https://www.linkedin.com/in/somiro-wellness-069632196/
https://www.facebook.com/profile.php?id=61556585490023
https://www.instagram.com/somirowellness/
https://www.somirowellness.ca/

I've been a social worker for 22 years, with 18 of those spent as a Mental Health and Addictions Worker. In 2019, I launched my private practice, offering life coaching and therapy services. I'm a proud mom of three amazing kids, and married to a wonderful husband who supports all my wild ideas and adventures. I love being creative and spending time outdoors—whether it's at the beach, in the woods, or hiking in the mountains. Board games, beach days and hiking with my family are my go-to for downtime. I am a proud Canadian and love to travel when I can. I like most things "hippy-dippy" and take a holistic approach to therapy. I'm passionate about sharing what I know so people can empower themselves and create lives filled with more joy. And yes—I practice what I preach because I know these strategies really work!

Happiness Is in the Details

By Jennifer Andrews, BSW, RSW

I followed all the rules (well, most of them). Doesn't that mean I should be happy? I graduated high school, went to university, earned a Bachelor of Arts in Sociology, eventually attended a second university and graduated with a Bachelor of Social Work, stayed out of trouble, found a job with great benefits and a good pension, found my Prince Charming, got married, had babies—now wasn't I supposed to "live Happily Ever After?" I thought so. Aren't those the unwritten societal rules we're all led to believe as we grow up? Do all the right things and you'll live a happy grown-up life? What a pile of bullshit! Don't you think?

After procrastinating in true Jen style, I sat down to write this chapter. This means I checked Facebook and Instagram, debated joining a Masterclass, and then settled on some meditation music for focus and productivity. I decided to Google the definition of "to defy." The first result was the Oxford Dictionary, and the very first line read: "openly resist or refuse to obey." The example they used in a sentence was "a woman who defies convention." I thought that was interesting since I had Googled the word out of curiosity before writing my chapter for a book composed of all-women authors sharing their stories about defying something! I took that as a good sign.

Similar words in that definition included resist, withstand, take a stand against, hold out against, and stand up to. I thought that was cool. If anything, I hope you learn from this chapter that you can be a good person and still take a stand against or stand up to or resist anything in your life that crosses your boundaries. I don't mean using boundaries to manipulate others or create an abusive situation. I mean boundaries designed to protect you and your values so you can create a happier, more fulfilled life for yourself.

I was in my late thirties, early forties perhaps (I'm not great with exact dates), and I remember crying in our living room and telling my husband, "It is not fair! We followed all the rules! We did things in the order we were 'supposed to.' Why do we keep struggling? Why are we always behind everyone else!" At that time, it felt like everyone else was buying new homes, going on trips, building successful businesses, and getting ahead in life. I felt stuck and angry. I was not feeling fulfilled or particularly happy. I had happy moments and joyful experiences, but overall, something wasn't quite right. You could say it was depression, but that didn't quite fit either. It was something different. I also told him, "I KNOW we are meant for more! I know it is out there; I can feel it! It's so close!" I truly believed it. I really could feel it.

The funny thing is, I was working as a therapist at a Mental Health and Addictions Clinic at the time. I had already been there for a while. When I first started, I loved it. It was such a great job. The team of therapists I worked with were wonderful—kind, smart, successful, confident people who were very passionate about what they did and the people they helped every day. We were given lots of educational opportunities and events. Not to mention, it had a good pension, great benefits, and decent vacation time (part of the goals of being a grown-up were completed all in one spot). It was ironic that I was feeling as crappy as I was, yet I was teaching other people how to create healthier habits, mindsets, coping strategies, and more to build a happier, more joy-filled life.

The sad thing about the great job was that management started to change, then the environment shifted, and eventually, some people moved on, altering the team dynamic. It became a toxic place to be. The problem with toxic environments is that you don't always see the toxins spreading. I let that toxicity bleed into other areas of my life, filling my soul with a heavy cloud of poison. Except it wasn't poison; it was my own mindset and my failure to respect and protect my boundaries. It was me.

At first, when I made that realization, I was like, "WTF!" and thought, "How could I have let this happen?" I teach this stuff to people, for crying out loud! After some crying, self-blame, and maybe a small dose of "How could I be so stupid!" I wiped the tears away and realized that if I wanted something different, I had to do something different. After all, isn't doing the same thing over and over again expecting different results the definition of insanity? I started to get excited because it was something I could change!

The first thing I remember is being blatantly aware that I thought I was practicing what I was teaching, but obviously, I was not doing a good job at it. I recall seeing a workshop for a Masterclass by a man named Robin S. Sharma through the Mindvalley Group and thought, what the heck, I signed up for it. I enjoyed his presentation and took copious notes, which was silly because I ended up buying his book that the class was based on and read it too. It was called *The 5 AM Club*. Again, kind of ironic because I was NOT a morning person. But I reminded myself that if I wanted to be different, I needed to do different. So, I jumped in. 5 AM. I also remember thinking that it was such an ungodly hour to get up! I mean, come on, I am not a farmer, baker, or fisherman! But there I was, getting my ass up at 5 AM to do the 20/20/20 routine! That routine was 20 minutes of moving, 20 minutes of meditating, and 20 minutes of writing. Not only was I getting up at a stupid o'clock in the morning, but now I was going to do things instead of drinking coffee and waiting for my eyes to pop open.

It was hard at first. My attention span was shorter than Danny DeVito—how could I meditate for 20 minutes? And what on earth was I going to write about for that long? Moving was okay, surprisingly. I would go for a walk or do yoga or stretches, and I fell into that easily. Meditation took a lot longer to get used to, but I chose guided meditations on YouTube and gradually could listen to them longer and longer. Now, I look forward to doing meditations that are almost an hour long. The writing—now that one I am super proud of. At first, I would just journal or write some goals or jot down things I wanted to let go of. But then I started a gratitude journal. That, I fell in love with.

You see, gratitude is a feeling that releases dopamine and serotonin. Those chemical friends are part of a system that makes us feel pleasure and happiness. Plus, in the energy field of it all, being in a state of gratitude will attract more things into your life that will make you feel even more grateful. It is a beautiful cycle. That's putting it simply for the sake of the chapter's length, but that's it in a nutshell. I even challenged myself to never write the same thing twice in my gratitude journal for a whole year. I am very proud to say that I did it. Now, don't get me wrong, I would often say that I was grateful for my kids or my husband, but it was always very specific. And those specific things were always different. For instance, I am grateful that Devin made me tea when he knew I was cold. Or how grateful I was that my kids laughed so hard at the story we told. Or how grateful I was that I could make the changes I needed to create the happiness that I craved. The happiness is in the details.

I wish I could tell you that it was that simple and easy. Wouldn't it be grand if we could do the 20/20/20 for a year and then be spectacularly happy? Or if there were a real magic wand? Sadly, there isn't. I made a mindful effort to truly start practicing what I taught my clients. I took the advice I gave to others and set better boundaries, used more emotion regulation skills, became aware of my triggers without guilt and shame, and changed how I reacted to them. I would ask myself, "Would I want my kids to react this way? How do I want to be a role model for them so they can see healthy behaviors in action?" At work, I asked myself, "How would a leader respond?" I could still feel passionate about a topic or boundary, but I didn't always have to get distressed about it. I practiced letting go of what I could not control and took the reins of what I could.

During that changing season of my life, I had some aha moments about my beliefs and thoughts. One of my core beliefs was that I was stupid. Yup, I said it. I am stupid. How could I be so stupid? Why would I do something so stupid? What a stupid thing to do! And just to change it up a bit, I would throw in the words dumb or dumbass instead. Once I had kids, I told myself I was not going to say things to myself that I wouldn't say to my children. I was good at asking myself this question: "Would I say this to my kids?" If not, then I had to rephrase it. However, that stupid belief just hung on like a baby possum hitching a ride for life! No matter how I phrased it, the result was the same. I was calling myself stupid.

I didn't have the best grades growing up. I had to study for tests and never made A's. I do not know my times tables off by heart (yes, even at 50). I don't seem to have the capability to use witty comebacks when I'm faced with a sassy comment in the moment. I was in the math class we called low math. I often felt like I was never as smart as most of the people I hung out with, just to name a few. However, in line with my new goal to practice what I teach, I decided it was time to face it. I was smart. It took a long time to work through that one. The biggest way I broke that habit was by looking for evidence that I was smart! Guess what? I have lots and lots of evidence! Including, I don't know what I don't know. It is amazing how much compassion I have when I make a mistake now. Occasionally, the feeling of being stupid tries to work its way back in, but I shut it down quickly because I know it is not true. It's just old habits hanging around again.

In all that hullabaloo, I noticed that many of the triggers and beliefs were seeds that grew from my past and childhood experiences that I thought I had sorted through but obviously weren't completely resolved. I couldn't blame my unhappiness with life all on a toxic workplace. I needed to reevaluate some relationships, face some hard truths about certain people in my life, process some events that occurred, and make necessary changes to move forward with my goals.

It took time, and things changed over the years. I got my own therapist to help me sort things out. I let go of resentments and embraced a version of life that made more room for gratitude and fun. In July of 2022, I quit the full-time, great-benefit, five-week-vacation, very secure job to open my own wellness practice. My dream was to open a practice that incorporated multiple modalities of healing: mental health therapy, massage therapy, chiropractic services, reiki, and other healing modalities that fit the vision. I wanted to show people that they could empower themselves to create healthier lives and not have to wait until they were sick or hurt to seek help; they could take proactive measures. They could have other healing modalities to complement the Western medicine that is so valuable to our society today. I was so excited! My husband and I used a lot of our own money to renovate a rented office space. I made five usable offices, and they were bright and welcoming. The plan was to rent out the other offices to practitioners who shared my dream. I was scheduled to open in October 2022. It was going to be great! My dream, my own business, my own hours! I was showing my kids that you can have a dream and make it a reality!

Then, the challenges arrived in ways I never, ever anticipated or planned for. In August of 2022, my dad was diagnosed with cancer. He had been unwell, going for tests and scans. I had a suspicion it was cancer, but the news hit me like a truck. In January of 2023, my husband was diagnosed with cancer—two different kinds, totally unrelated. I didn't see that one coming. Tests and treatments for both followed the news. I cried a lot, shook it off, took deep breaths, then refocused my mind on the next thing that needed to be done, whether it was in my business, driving to appointments, or supporting my dad and husband with their treatments. I embraced gratitude like my life depended on it. I was grateful I had the flexibility to help where and when I could. I was grateful that I could spend time with my dad. I was grateful for the immense support I had and still have from family and friends. In the following months, my grandmother's cancer returned as well. By then, it felt like everything was a blur, and all I could do was focus on the very next step and be grateful for whatever I could. I allowed myself to feel the scary, sad, dark feelings, but I couldn't get stuck there. I needed to be present for my family, my kids, and myself. Unfortunately, I was not there for my business. It did not get the attention it needed to thrive.

We lost Dad in September of 2023. It was so hard. Grief sucks big floppy donkey dink. It's so weird because I logically know he is gone, and yet two nights ago, I was driving home from work and thought I should call him to see how his day was going. When those things happen, sometimes I smile, thinking he would laugh at me. Sometimes, I cry because I miss him.

On May 6th, 2024, I lost my beautiful office space. I was evicted because I couldn't keep up with the rent. Five offices were a big space, and I only had myself and two part-time renters in the building. I was so upset and so embarrassed. Due to the level of embarrassment I felt, I told very few people. It was a secret I kept for months.

On May 16th, we lost my grandma. I could not believe the way things were going. It was shocking and emotionally draining. Gratitude again was still my friend. I was grateful I was able to spend time with my grandma in the weeks leading up to her passing. I was grateful for that large group of support again. I was grateful that the treatment regimen my husband had and continues to have, fighting cancer's ugly presence in our lives.

I am grateful for the colleague I was introduced to who shares her office space with me without hesitation. I am grateful for the part-time job I found at a Family Health Team that helps keep a roof over our family's heads. I am grateful for the clients who continue to see me ongoing and new. I am grateful for the cute snoring sounds my dog makes as she sleeps beside me while I type. I am grateful for finally being able to settle things with my office landlord and move on. I am grateful for the new office space I found in another wellness center. I am grateful I will only be responsible for one room and not the entire place. I am grateful that

I took a week-long business course through our local small business center. I am grateful I took the time to create a new business plan for a virtual therapy company. I am grateful for the grant I won to help me launch that branch of my company. I am grateful for my partner in this wild ride and his love and support through all we have been through. I am grateful for my children's blooming curiosity and stories.

I am grateful I took the time to rephrase my thoughts and beliefs and create new habits. I know without a shadow of a doubt that my most recent mindset helped me get through the past few years. I still get angry. I still get sad. I still get overwhelmed. I just don't get stuck there anymore. I give it a hug and kiss it goodbye.

I have made peace with losing the first office space. I don't want the trials and tribulations of life to hold me down. I don't want to give up on my dream because it did not go the way I planned. I am certain this next chapter won't go as planned either. At the same time, building resiliency is about growing stronger in the face of adversity. I would like to think that building resiliency also embraces the concept of defying convention.

Natalie Horseman

Horseman Publishing
Nurse | Author | Coach

https://www.instagram.com/the40yearoldwriter
www.horsemanbooks.com

Natalie Horseman, MSN, RN, is a dedicated nurse with nearly two decades of experience in child and family development. Her extensive background in healthcare has equipped her with a profound understanding of resilience and strength. Throughout her career, Natalie has been committed to guiding individuals through life's most challenging moments with both compassion and empathy. Her personal journey of overcoming adversity has deeply fueled her passion for empowering others. Through her writing, Natalie combines practical advice with heartfelt encouragement, creating a sense of community for those navigating life's storms. She believes that while our experiences shape us, they do not define us. Through her contributions, Natalie strives to inspire readers to embrace their inner strength and resilience, offering reassurance that they are never alone on their journey.

Kaleidoscope

By Natalie Horseman

The Mosaic

When you look back on your life, where does your mind wander? Do you trace the early days—childhood, adolescence, and beyond—connecting the dots between who you were and who you've become? Or do you anchor your thoughts to a singular moment—college, marriage, the birth of a child? Maybe you turn away from the past entirely, eyes fixed on the horizon, moving forward with resolve, leaving what's behind in the dust.

For me, reflection is a different kind of journey. When I look back, I don't see a continuous thread, but a fractured mosaic of memories, sharp and scattered. Some pieces burn with light—joy, love, hope—and others are darkened by the shadows of past pain. These shards, each carrying its own weight of fear, guilt, and regret, pull me into a time I can't escape, yet can't seem to leave behind.

Once, this mosaic was whole—a radiant thing, glowing with purpose. It was a kaleidoscope of colors, each piece brilliant in its own way, casting beams of light that stretched out in every direction. But over time, cracks began to form, creeping unnoticed at first, then widening. Slowly, the light dimmed, and the whole began to fragment. Each fracture told the story of loss, of trauma, each one slowly chipping away at the foundation.

Unconsciously, I boxed away each broken piece—shelving them in the corners of my mind, out of sight and out of reach. These were the dark pieces, the parts of me I refused to touch. I thought that by locking them away, I could protect myself from the pain. But in truth, I was only disconnecting from the past, pretending it wasn't there. To the outside world, I became the epitome of strength—fiercely independent, a nurse who climbed the ladder, redefined her career, and thrived in the art of reinvention. With each step forward, I drifted further into the shadows, hiding the cracks beneath a mask of unbreakable strength.

For years, I believed silence was strength. I thought that by hiding the broken pieces behind a smile, I was resilient. I kept my boxes closed, my mess hidden, convinced it was my burden to bear alone. But silence was never strength—it was survival. I had survived, yes, but I hadn't truly lived.

This is the story of my journey, the path from survival to transformation, from silence to strength. If you've ever felt like you were running from yourself, I hope my story can help guide you back to the truth of who you really are.

Armour of Silence

I was raised by a strong, independent woman who never wavered in all of life's storms. From her, I learned early on how to stand tall and weather the fiercest winds of adversity. Growing up, I became skilled at reading people, sensing what wasn't said, and anticipating the unspoken reactions that often followed. In that constant tension, I perfected the art of hiding my feelings—locking them away, far out of reach. Talking about emotions wasn't just unnecessary; it felt dangerous. Instead, I wore a smile like armor and carried on, no matter the weight I bore beneath the surface. Even as a child, I guarded my heart against disappointment, holding myself together amidst the storm of fear, uncertainty, and pain.

When a devastating tragedy struck my family, it altered our lives forever. Sudden, all-consuming, and profound, it exposed us to a depth of loss, chaos, and turmoil that I hadn't known existed. I watched as it shattered our world, leaving cracks in my home and deep, unhealable wounds across my family. It felt as though we were left to pick up the broken pieces, but no matter how hard we tried, we could never put them back together. In that moment, I learned the brutal art of compartmentalizing—burying grief, loss, and fear in tightly sealed boxes deep within me. I adopted the lesson from my mother's strength: vulnerability wasn't an option. You simply moved forward. You kept going.

I learned survival. I learned what it meant to endure, to persist in the face of overwhelming loss. And those lessons—buried beneath layers of resilience—became the foundation upon which I built my life.

The Weight of Silence

Growing up in a family marked by divorce, I never had an example of what a strong, supportive partnership could be. The relationships I witnessed around me were marred by dysfunction, where miscommunication festered, and anger and hurt seemed to linger in the air, often giving way to bitterness that seeped into every interaction. I didn't know that relationships weren't meant to be filled with chaos, overwhelming emotions, and constant fear and pain. To me, this was just normal—the light and dark sides of relationships intertwined.

I thought love was about sacrifice and endurance, and I had learned to mistake silence for strength. So when the relationship I was in turned toxic, I stayed. It started with small, subtle signs—control disguised as concern, possessiveness masked as love. But over time, those red flags grew bolder, escalating from mental and emotional manipulation to physical abuse.

Looking back, I realize how deeply that experience warped my understanding of love. I confused pain with loyalty, and the scars I carried from those years tainted every relationship that came after. I had become desensitized to the chaos—the tears, the emotional outbursts, the promises of change followed by more violence. It was a cycle that became so predictable I learned to brace myself for the next rampage, convinced that after each storm, the kindness and the "I'm sorry" would mean things were finally different. But they never were.

I never told anyone. Not my family, not my friends. I convinced myself it was my mess to fix, believing that I had somehow deserved it. With each blow—whether a cruel word or a shove—I sank deeper into silence, thinking if I was better, prettier, smarter, or more obedient, it would stop. I internalized the blame, convincing myself that if I could change, I could fix what was broken. I didn't realize the problem was never me. Slowly, I started losing pieces of myself, accepting the notion that this was all I was worth. The shame and isolation crushed me, but I still clung to the hope that if I could just be different, things might change. What I failed to see at the time was that the more I tried to fix it, the more of myself I lost.

That relationship dragged on for years, a brutal cycle of fleeting hope followed by gut-wrenching lows. Time and time again, I returned, foolishly clinging to the belief that this time, he would change—that the violence would stop. But one day, it all came crashing down. We were in the front yard, trapped in yet another explosive argument. He gripped a gun in his hand, but there was no shock. For years, that weapon had been his constant, twisted companion, appearing without warning, always with the same chilling purpose: to terrorize, to dominate, to break me. It wasn't just a tool of fear—it was a weapon he used to twist my heart, threatening his own life to make me feel guilty, to keep me chained in this toxic cycle. But this time, I didn't fight back. I was too shattered, too drained, too far gone—physically, mentally, and emotionally—to care about the outcome. I stood there, hollow and numb, and with a voice void of all defiance, I said, "Just do it. I don't care anymore."

At that moment, I didn't know what was going to happen—whether one of us would walk away, or if neither of us would. I had lost all sense of control, not knowing if I would survive what was about to unfold. I was too tired to fight, too worn out to care. After years of trying to outrun him during his rampages, years of covering bruises and hiding my brokenness, I was completely drained. I had desperately clung to the hope that things would change, but I was exhausted, physically and emotionally. Miraculously, that moment marked the end of his power over me. The relationship ended, and I should have felt free, but I was left with an emptiness I couldn't shake. I had left him behind, but the scars from those years followed me relentlessly.

After so many years trapped in that cycle, I no longer knew who I was without it. My identity had become so entwined with chaos and survival that without it, I was a shell of myself—lost and uncertain of how to move forward. The shadow of my past followed me, haunting every step, as I struggled to rebuild a life that felt foreign and unclaimed. The deep, lingering scars loomed over every attempt I made to forge a new path and reclaim my sense of self.

Interrupting the Silence

After the relationship ended, I did what I had always done—I boxed up my trauma, burying it deep in the recesses of my mind. The memories, the pain, the guilt—all of it was shoved into the furthest corners, hidden away as if locking it out would somehow make it disappear. And then I threw myself into my career. Nursing became my refuge, my escape. It allowed me to focus on the suffering of others while I numbed my own. Promotions came easily, each one a fleeting salve for wounds I refused to acknowledge. But no amount of success could mask the emptiness inside me.

For 15 years, I ran. I ran from the pain, from the past, from the truth I was terrified to face. I believed that if I just worked hard enough, climbed high enough, I could outrun the darkness. But like poison seeping through the cracks, burnout slowly crept in, and by the time I realized it had taken hold, I was deep in the darkness—completely lost, my sense of direction shattered, and further from myself than I had ever been.

I spent those years living a lie. On the outside, I was the healer, the one who helped others mend. But inside, I was unraveling, haunted by the ghosts of past mistakes, toxic relationships, and pain I had long buried. It wasn't until I started therapy that I was forced to confront the depth of my trauma. Each session was a journey into the rubble of my past. My therapist gently guided me through the process of unearthing the boxes I had sealed tight, one layer at a time. It was terrifying. I had spent so many years building walls around my emotions, and now, I had to tear them down, brick by brick. I had to learn to be vulnerable, to admit that I wasn't okay, and to ask for help.

One of the hardest lessons I had to learn was how to take off my "running shoes." For years, I had fled at the first sign of conflict, discomfort, or vulnerability. I had convinced myself that if I could just leave before things got messy, I could protect myself from heartache. My life was a series of exits—relationships, jobs, dreams—always bracing myself for the moment when I'd feel trapped again.

But the truth was, my constant flight only deepened the emptiness. Superficial relationships became my refuge, and real intimacy, my greatest fear. I had convinced myself that if I controlled the exit, I could avoid the inevitable heartbreak. Yet, each time I ran, the wound only festered, the pain lingering longer, the isolation growing deeper.

Therapy shattered this illusion of safety. I had to face the truth: running never shielded me from pain; it only prolonged it. Vulnerability, the very thing I had always feared, was the path to healing. I had to learn that courage wasn't in fleeing—it was in staying, in confronting the discomfort head-on.

Learning to communicate openly was a monumental shift. It meant expressing my emotions even when it felt like I was exposing my soul. It meant asking for help when I felt weakest, admitting that I wasn't okay. This journey wasn't quick, nor was it painless. There were moments of doubt, times when I wanted to retreat into old habits and shut down. The fear that history would repeat itself loomed large, an ever-present shadow.

But slowly, as I dismantled the walls I had spent years building, a new path began to emerge. I found my voice. I started to speak up, to advocate for my needs in relationships instead of retreating into silence. I began to believe that I deserved love—not because I could avoid pain, but because I was worthy of it in my brokenness.

The rebuilding process is still ongoing. There are still days when the fear of being trapped again claws at my chest, when I want to bolt and hide. But each step forward is a victory. I'm learning that true strength lies in the courage to stay—stay with myself, stay with others, and embrace the messiness of life. It's in this act of staying present, of being authentic even when it's terrifying, that I'm finding my peace. The fear doesn't disappear, but it no longer has the power to control me. This is my journey of rediscovery, of healing, and of learning to be whole again.

The Shattering

One of the greatest battles I've faced has been learning to feel at home in my own skin. For years, I carried an invisible weight—shame and judgment about my appearance that consumed me from the inside out. Mirrors were my enemy, reflecting a version of myself I couldn't bear to acknowledge. Every glance felt like an accusation, a reminder of how I despised the way I looked. I couldn't shake the belief that no one could ever see me as beautiful; I couldn't even see it in myself. This struggle went far beyond vanity—it shaped the way I moved through the world and determined how I measured my worth.

For years, I tried to hide from the world, wrapping myself in layers of clothing and avoiding anything that might expose me. I shrank from social situations, refusing to let anyone see me—truly see me—because I feared they would judge me the way I judged myself. Shame became my constant companion, an invisible cloak that weighed me down with every step. I was convinced that the world saw me through the same lens of disgust that I used to view myself.

Yet, part of my healing has been about confronting that shame, peeling it back layer by painful layer. I'm not fully there yet—I still have days when self-acceptance feels just out of reach. But I'm learning to approach my body with less judgment, seeing it not as a collection of flaws, but as a testament to strength and survival. I've come to understand that beauty is not a singular standard—it's a spectrum, a collection of all the things that make me uniquely me. What I've realized is that the way I view myself is often harsher than how others see me.

Through therapy, I began to challenge those long-held beliefs and started to recognize the resilience my body represents. It carries me through every challenge, enduring and adapting in ways I never gave it credit for. And more than that, I've come to see that my worth is not defined by the shape of my body or the scars I've hidden, but by my character, my kindness, and my experiences. I am not my imperfections. I am the woman who has survived them. In this process, I've shattered the way I once saw myself, and in its place, I'm creating a beautiful and chaotic mosaic that is uniquely me—imperfect, whole, and endlessly evolving.

This journey is ongoing, and I'm not finished yet—there are still days when self-acceptance feels elusive. But with every step forward, I am learning to love the body I once rejected. I'm learning to see it not as a burden, but as a part of me, worthy of kindness and care. True self-acceptance doesn't come from how I look; it comes from embracing every part of who I am—scars and all.

The Author

For so long, I believed my past had already written the ending of my story. The trauma, the pain, the shame—I thought they were the chapters that defined me. But now I see the truth: our past is not the conclusion. It is a part of us, yes, but it doesn't have to control us. In the process of healing, I found myself—my voice, my strength, and the power to rewrite my story. We are not bound by the weight of our histories. We hold the power to reshape our narratives, to choose a different path—even after we've been broken beyond recognition.

Healing isn't about erasing the past. It's about learning to carry it differently. By releasing the false belief that our worst moments define us, we can recognize the strength forged in the fire of those very struggles. I am not the woman I was in those years of silence and suffering. I've found my voice, and in doing so, I've realized that vulnerability is not a weakness—it is the ultimate act of courage. Asking for help doesn't make us fragile; it makes us human.

We are never powerless in the face of our pain. We have the ability to confront it, to learn from it, and to transform it into something that strengthens us. The journey to healing is rarely smooth—it's filled with setbacks and moments of despair, often feeling like two steps forward, one step back. But every inch of that journey is worth it. You don't need to be perfect or have it all figured out. And you certainly don't have to walk this path alone.

If you're feeling weighed down by your past or burdened by the scars you carry, remember this: you are not alone. Within your pain lies incredible strength, and in your resilience, there is profound beauty. The road ahead may be long, but it's worth every step. Each new day is an opportunity to reclaim your story and rewrite it on your own terms.

Take every piece of your journey and weave it into the beautiful kaleidoscope of your life—a one-of-a-kind masterpiece that reflects your growth, strength, and transformation. Every piece matters, and together, they form the vibrant tapestry of who you are becoming. You are more than your past. You are the author of your own life, and no one—not even your history—can take that power away from you.

So, keep going. Keep healing. You are worthy of every step of this journey. No matter where you've been, the power to shape your future is always in your hands. You are worth every step of the journey—just as I am, just as we all are.

Shannon Pereira

Powered By Mushrooms
Microdosing Coach, Speaker / Trainer, Writer

https://www.linkedin.com/in/shannon-pereira-4391ab28\
https://www.facebook.com/shannon.pereira2
https://www.instagram.com/poweredbymushroomscoaching/
http://www.poweredbymushroomscoaching.com/
https://www.youtube.com/@PowerPerspectivesWithShannon11

Shannon Pereira is a Microdosing Mushroom Consciousness Coach, a Speaker & Trainer as well as a content creator and writer. While yoga, psychedelic study and meditation are her passions, she thrives while helping others reactive their SUPER-POWER. She believes ALL of our SUPER-POWERS are the ability to shift and evolve our perspectives. She believes in having fun in life and implements an 'Enlighten the FK Up,' playful approach to regulate the nervous system and transform the lives of her clients, students, teams or corporate leadership communities. Her books, "Powered By Mushrooms – an Anthology," and "The Power Perspectives Pathway: 7 Transformative Principles to Activate Your Super-Power & Enlighten the FK Up" are in the birthing process and will arrive near to the end of 2025. Reach out to connect. She'd love to hear from you!

The Cyclops & the Amazon

By Shannon Pereira

"Circumstances do not determine your state of being. Your state of being determines your circumstances."
—**Bashar / Darryl Anka**

On November 29, 2018, I woke up in a Sydney hospital emergency ward, safe from a dangerous infection, but without my right breast.

> *I had jogged to work again. It was another 7 kilometres with 2 bras on because I wouldn't acknowledge the series of stabbing, shooting pains in my right breast.*
>
> *I had read many alternative healing resources, attended healing seminars like Dr. Joe Dispenza's Advanced workshop, became certified in Advanced Theta Healing, Dr. Joe Vitale's Ho'Oponopono Healing, completed multiple yoga teacher trainings and more.*
>
> *Yet my shallow ego, in needing to believe that I could heal myself, was answered by the Universe with, "And so shall you continue to need."*
>
> *Like most of us, I just didn't know what I had to experience to become who I am. And like ALL moments of hindsight clarity, I didn't know then what I know now.*

Shortly after I arrived at my workplace and changed into my corporate attire, I thought I must have inadvertently spilled tea on my shirt. Upon changing again, I understood this was not tea – but a bloody, infected fluid seeping from two bras and out into the world – jolting me to the realization that my implant had ruptured, and my thinned flesh was too weak to hold it.

The beautiful intention of my body was to get this foreign invader immediately out of it. And for that, I will be forever grateful. But at the time, in the hustle culture I subscribed to, I didn't have time for this. I had two more meetings that day and looming deadlines.

Now, the thought of placing my health as a tertiary priority behind a worldwide corporation's bottom dollar is preposterous – but like many humans, I was lost under the veil of societal pressures and expectations.

When I awoke later that night in the hospital's emergency ward, my right breast, both the implant and significant breast tissue, was gone. The left one, still intact, sat perched alone and perplexed as to where its mate had gone.

My ability to put my usual, positively programmed spin on the situation was in the trash – near to a bloody and burst implant, no doubt.

I was alone. I was scared. And I was quickly descending into the depths of my self-dug pity pit.

What awoke me that night in the ER was not the searing pain from hastened incisions and subsequent stitches.

It also *wasn't* the new definition of "deformed" I now had attached to me via my hospital-issued paperwork. As I contemplated the meaning of deformed, "mutilated, contorted, damaged," it became a word I would continue to let penetrate my self-meaning and suck tears from my heart repeatedly throughout those first hours.

And what woke me that night was not the nauseating thought of the awards ceremony I was elected to emcee in 2 weeks. I was already highly anxious about the speeches I'd be making to more than 80 work colleagues and their partners. But now, thinking how my dress wouldn't fit anymore, and that people might call me 'Cyclops Boob' behind my back, had my guts churning.

It's okay to laugh at 'Cyclops Boob,' by the way. It's quite the mental image, right? Like, if my remaining left breast somehow became centred, maybe it would gain the ability to shoot lasers or send and receive telepathic messages? So far – nada.

Waking Up

> *"When you change the way you look at things, the things you look at change."*
> —**Dr. Wayne Dwyer, The Power of Intentions**

Let me tell you what *did* wake me up that night in the emergency ward.

It was the urgent, sombre sound of violent coughing and desperate gasping for air.

It was my ER neighbour to my left. It was frightening for me, so I can only imagine what she was going through.

She couldn't have been more than 65, frail, afraid, and fighting for her life in a sterile, cold hospital room, comforted only by strangers, all wishing their circumstances were different.

Before I could find my emergency buzzer, a nurse was already on the way.

After some swift medicating, my neighbour settled down. Her breathing graduated into a dry, labour-intensive anxiety as opposed to the literal battle for each moment it had been mere minutes before.

In a brief but bone-chilling conversation, I learned that the retching and fighting for air would continue for the remainder of her life, interrupted only by enough medication to sedate her.

I learned she was just waiting until a family member came.

And I learned that she had no expectation of leaving that hospital alive.

After the gut-wrenching defeat of that understanding, wanting to hug her, hold her hand, and tell her it was going to be okay, I just lay in my bed and tried to soften my panic as she drifted off with the help of what I can only speculate to be copious amounts of morphine.

They say, *'comparison is the thief of joy,'* and truly, I must agree with that, **unless** comparison is a reminder of gratitude's saving grace.

I remember taking long, deep, easily executed breaths – simply because I could.

After that, it became increasingly difficult to dig my pity pit much deeper.

But of course, in between the nurse's blood pressure check-ins, and loud machines beeping at all hours, my fragile mind would return to its newly devolved self-definitions of 'deformed, unworthy, Cyclops Boob'.

Like many vulnerable women who have been seductively, intentionally taught to dislike their natural bodies by social media, the entertainment industry, and you name it, I thought if I could just fix my 'ugly, misshapen, not good enough' self, then I could be much more attractive and finally have the confidence necessary to be 'seen'.

And so, as a 20-something-year-old – I took my savings to a strange doctor, in a strange land with a strange protocol to slice open my beautiful, pure flesh and fill it with inflated silicon balloons so that I could feel 'seen'.

Trigger Warning: In absolutely no way am I looking down on cosmetic or plastic surgeries. Try as I might, how could I assume to know the world through another's individual perspective? How could I know the unique journey each person has on their way to self-love?

But trying to fit in *or* trying to stand out by such forceful, unnatural procedures now just sounds bizarre. It sounds like a sickened and unwell society that promotes implanting foreign materials before it promotes mental health, body-positive education, and self-love.

I often imagine explaining cosmetic surgery to a flabbergasted extraterrestrial that would descend through a series of asking "Why?" and not come out any more enlightened on the matter.

Pain & Synchronicity – Unexpected Teachers

"The wound is the place where the light enters you."
—**Rumi**

Pain can be a very powerful teacher – one reserved for the humbling of healing hearts. Thankfully, pain *and* synchronicity were both to be my teachers.

And so, lying in the ER, I let my anxious thoughts drift to this awards night I'd be emceeing. In an effort to prevent 'Cyclops Boob' from catching on at the office, I thought to order a prosthetic breast insert from an online store like Amazon.

I typed into my search engine, "AMAZON RIGHT BREAST", and what happened next was so simple and yet so spectacularly profound that it changed my life and ensured my endless appreciation for the magic of the Universe's Divine Intelligence.

On my phone now were not images of lumpy breast-shaped bits, promising to arrive in a timely manner, as I had expected.

Instead, I was now staring at images and links to tales of the legendary AMAZONS!!!

From ancient Greek, the word "a" means *without,* and "mazoa" means *breast.* The Amazons were said to battle with the strength and courage of men and yet, known to be even fiercer.

They were infamous for cutting away or cauterizing their right breasts so that they could be better archers, hunters, and providers for their tribe!

They were WARRIORS! They were fighters – not for glory or for fame, but because IT WAS IN THEIR BLOOD AND HEARTS TO BE!

I was astounded!

What made this even more extraordinary was the fact that, like many women (and many men), I was having a Gal Gadot / Wonder Woman crush at the time. The Wonder Woman movie had recently come out of theatres, and Gadot's Amazonian, 'love above all else' portrayal was effortless to adore.

So much so, that in practicing emoting and harnessing the feelings of strength, confidence, and power, I had put the image of her, as the Amazonian Wonder Woman in battle, on my vision board and my *Mind Movie*.

(If you're unaware, a Mind Movie is an incredibly effective tool for manifestation. Picture your personalised vision board images moving to your favourite, most inspiring song, with text and affirmations written by you, and for you, specific to your goals and desires. It is ideally watched upon falling asleep / or upon waking, when the brain is in theta brainwaves. This is known to be when the doors to the subconscious mind are most open to new neural programming.)

In my Mind Movie, which I'd only made one month earlier for Dr. Joe Dispenza's workshop, **it was the exact image** of Gal Gadot as Wonder Woman that I was now looking at on my phone in the ER ward, solely from the search to find a prosthetic insert on Amazon.

It was the image that I had intentionally worked towards!

You never know how you will manifest something. Most of the time, it will come as a complete shock but simultaneously be exactly what you asked for and with a wisdom you couldn't have known prior.

This is the unfathomable love of the Divine Dichotomy. Finding evolution and empowerment through discomfort and pain, how exquisite!

And just like that, my perspective had dramatically shifted and evolved!

PERSPECTIVE IS EVERYTHING!

> *"We can complain because rose bushes have thorns or rejoice because thorns have roses."*
> —**Alphonse Karr, Letter from My Garden**

Charles Swindoll's timeless quote, **"Life is 10% what happens to you and 90% how you react to it**," offers a challenging reminder of its powerful truth every time I feel my feet slip dangerously near the proverbial mountain's edge.

Herein lies the power of choice.

I could choose to be a sad, deformed 30-something, 'Cyclops Boob,' alone and undesirable,

OR

I could choose to be a mission-driven Amazonian Wonder Woman (but with decidedly less man-murdering – almost none).

My choice was obvious. It felt wonderful to choose Wonder Woman.

But that doesn't mean I didn't have to keep choosing that perspective every time I saw myself topless, or every time my insert had obviously moved out of place in public, or every time I thought about the explanation I'd have to provide a potential romantic interest.

It's necessary to stand firm in the decision to see from the perspective you prefer *again and again* until it is wired into your neural programming and, quite literally, becomes your preferred identity written into the language of your brain and body. This is a crucial part of the process of crossing the river change.

In life, we are the creators, writers, directors, and stars of our own life's great production. And in every moment, we get to decide. Do we want to be the victim or the victor? Either choice is accepted immediately when we make it, and either choice can be changed in just a moment.

The Ability to Shift & Evolve Our Perspectives Is Our Super Power!

"It's not what you look at that matters, it's what you see."
—**Henry David Thoreau**

If you're reading this, it's probable that your core values may be similar to mine: Love, Evolution, Spirituality.

And probably like you, in my ongoing quest to evolve and grow, I have taken many courses, read many books, interviewed thought leaders, and sat in many seminars and coaching sessions.

I've lived in ashrams, travelled the world for years with no home address, learned from shamanic healers, communed reverently with plant, amphibian, and fungi medicine, completed 1000+ hours of yoga teacher training, sat in silent meditation for days, sat in Satsang's with mystical psychics, studied hermetic philosophy, been electrocuted by the lightning of love that travelled through my spine from the cosmos and felt as if for just one unforgettable moment that Source energy looked my way.

What I've learned, and what I'm still learning, is that we can change the world we live in instantaneously if we want to and if we know how to, using the POWER of our PERSPECTIVES!

This has truly become a pathway for me. It's a path of the focused, cultivated resonance of vibration.

The PowerPerspectives Pathway

"You don't see the world as it is, you see it as you are."
—Anaïs Nin

Imagine journeying down your path, feeling empowered with tools and resources to be your most authentic, high-vibrational self; going as far as you can see and knowing that when you get there, you'll see further – exactly what you need. Imagining that journey for myself is what led me to create the ***PowerPerspectives Pathway***.

I want to share with you 7 remarkable principles that I've applied time and time again to harness the power of perspective and dramatically upgrade and enhance my life.

These principles can align you to your greater path with incredible side effects, including building greater resilience in the face of adversity, embodying ancient wisdom to delve deep into the mysteries of the Universe, and aligning your vibrational resonance to manifest more joy and peace.

These principles will work for anyone, anywhere, who wants to use the extreme rarity of the one thing they've got that no other being in the entire universe has – their perspective!

The foundational premise requires you to have an understanding that you are the only being in the entirety of existence that has your unique perspective.

No one can possibly see the world through your eyes. No one can possibly experience the way reality looks, sounds, feels, smells, tastes, etc. through your perception – but you.

That makes you *very* special. That makes you absolutely invaluable to 'All That Is', and 'All That Is' would be incomplete without you and your unfathomable You-ness.

Each of these 7 principles is more thoroughly broken down in my upcoming book, *The PowerPerspectives Pathway: 7 Transformative Principles to Activate Your Superpower & Enlighten the Fk Up.*

But here they are as a brief guide to get you thinking about just how powerful the way you see the world is.

1. Embody B.I.G. Energy

B.I.G. is an acronym for **B**alance, **I**ntention, and **G**ratitude.

Embodying Balance – In Hermetic Philosophy, balance is achieved through an understanding that polarities, rhythms, the ebb and flow of life, causation, effect, seasons, and genders may seem like exact opposites but are truly only parts of one ongoing cycle. Embodying balance asks us to keep "zooming out" when we are out of balance to see the bigger picture, which can enable us to "re-balance" or see we were never out of balance in the first place, only that our understanding or interpretation needed reevaluation as we move through our experiences.

Embodying Intention – Intention is everything. It's the trailer of the movie that you'd like your life to be. Visualization and imagination projected to the reality you prefer are paramount to the foundation of harnessing your superpower. Acting with intention is when we turn the thought into reality.

Embodying Gratitude – Expressing gratitude for what you already have and for what you wish to be yours, best communicates to the infinite field of potentiality that you are aligned with the receivership of that which you are grateful for. Genuine gratitude tells the Universe that you have a thing and are calling more of that into your field.

Effectively embodying B.I.G. Energy alone is enough to spiral your life into upward manifestation of whatever joys you can imagine. And you're always, all ways free to imagine anything.

2. Attune Your Vibrational Resonance

> *"Everything is energy and that's all there is to it. Match the frequency of the reality you want, and you cannot help but get that reality. It can be no other way. This is not philosophy. This is physics."*
> —**Albert Einstein**

Einstein's quote delves into quantum physics, the Observer Effect and collapsing the wave function of any potential into the physical, the particle, the reality you prefer to be a match to.

We were taught that if we first have a certain thing, then we can be or feel a certain way.

But we were taught incorrectly. Instead of wanting to "have" a thing (money, cars, houses, dream jobs, a lover) in order to "be" or feel a certain way (happy, fulfilled, joyous), vibrational resonance compels us to "be" in that vibrational state of being first, and then the "having" of that resonance will subsequently follow.

The quantum field, the universe, Source energy, whatever you call it, does not respond to what we want – it responds to who we're being.

3. Connect to Your Internal Navigation System

> *"Emotions are the most powerful force in the brain, and they dictate how we behave. True transformation begins when you realize that the power of change is in how you feel, not how you think."*
> —**Dr. Joe Dispenza**

At any given moment we can be still and ask our physiology, our emotional state of being – how we are feeling. Our emotions tell us immediately how we are responding to any stimulus.

If you are connected to this – by simply delving inward – we can shorten the refractory period of time spent in emotions we don't prefer, and with cultivated skills, opt for and feel more of the emotions we do want to feel.

4. Help Every One Every Where All At Once

> *"How wonderful it is that nobody need wait a single moment before starting to improve the world."*
> —**Anne Frank**

It sounds like much more work than it is.

When you send one love-filled expression of appreciation for 'All That Is,' or just beam unconditional love to yourself, a neighbour, or a stranger – you are raising the vibration of the collective conscious. That seemingly small act alone evolves humanity.

A decade ago, I committed to doing what I call, 3GD's or 3 Good Deeds A Day, and it has changed my life monumentally, and I'd like you to try it!

CALL TO ACTION:

Do one good deed a day for yourself as an act of self-love, because you cannot give from an empty cup (no one knows this better than parents).

Do one good deed a day for someone in your inner circle, a partner, family member, colleague, etc. (Chances are you're already doing this – but acknowledging this act and planning it accesses greater levels of empathy and compassion.)

Do one good deed a day for a stranger. It could be a smile or a compliment or just tuning in to someone's needs and asking, "Are you okay?" This small act has connected me to some of the most rewarding exchanges I've ever had.

5. Own Your Fear

"Fear is the result of resistance to the unknown. When you allow yourself to move through fear, you discover that the thing you feared the most was simply an illusion."
—**Bashar / Darryl Anka**

The **power** of *illusion* is the **illusion** of its *power*. If you're like me, perhaps contemplating this sentiment would have you lost, looking for the edge of the world to seek refuge in while you figured out which is power and which is illusion.

Fear operates in illusion.

Acknowledging that what we're afraid of is simply a reaction to an unknown outcome steeped in the potential of negative consequences. Acknowledging the illusion can help us face our fears with more courage and less need for control.

When we see fear as a valuable tool to understand that we're out of vibrational alignment with our higher selves, we can use it to identify and overcome a pre-programmed belief that no longer serves us.

If it is disempowering, it is fear. If it is empowering, it is the field in your true power.

And like Source energy, true power never needs to exert or prove itself. It cannot get offended, nor can it be anything else but truth.

6. Now Surrender

"Surrender means the courage to let go of what you think you need in order to embrace what's truly meant for you."
—**Joseph Campbell, The Hero's Journey**

When we can cut the ties from the 'Should Haves' and the 'Supposed to Bes' and simply surrender to following our bliss, without trying to please anyone else, miraculous things will happen.

People confuse surrender with weakness, but it takes a great deal of strength and inner-standing to allow and flow without forcing, pushing, or imposing your will.

This creates the necessary space for what is truly meant for you to come into your reality.

7. Enlighten the Fk Up!

> *"You don't stop playing because you get old. You get old because you stop playing."*
> —George Bernard Shaw

To play and to have fun are truly what makes this challenging journey worthwhile.

When we're stressed out, a state of being that is completely unnecessary but cultivated through societal pressures and unnatural expectations, we are not aligning with our purpose.

When we're in a state of homeostasis, cells in our bodies consistently die and are replaced with new cells. However, when we're consistently in a state of stress, the body is depleted and does not have expendable energy to nurture cellular regeneration. Cells that have died cannot be replenished. This means we're literally killing ourselves with worry, anxiety, and stress - all unnecessarily.

When we choose the perspective of light-heartedness and joviality, especially in the face of great turmoil and pain – we truly are levelling up and turning pain into purpose.

EACH ONE – REACH ONE; EACH ONE – TEACH ONE

The acronym for the 7 principles above is **E.A.C.H. O.N.E**. The concept of the acronym serves as a reminder of the best way in which we used to learn information – the tradition of storytelling.

If you can successfully explain any or all 7 principles of the PowerPerspectives Pathway to another, with your shifted and evolved narrative, then you've committed that information to your brain and are further embodying it by sharing it.

Telling <u>YOUR</u> story in the way that best serves you, is the work of an activated SUPERPOWER – the work of a perspective accurately aligned for both evolution of self and the collective.

You've also then successfully turned your pain into purpose-filled tools to expand and transform.

Wrapping It Up with a Bow

> *"The closer one gets to realizing his Personal Legend,*
> *the more that Personal Legend becomes*
> *his true reason for being."*
> —Paolo Coelho, The Alchemist

Recently having my other breast implant and tissue removed to free my body of a foreign article, to 'even out,' and to finally stop 'needing' to wear an insert, I'm struck by Paolo Coelho's timeless tale, *The Alchemist*.

Sometimes we need to ride the emotional rollercoaster of life that takes us far away from where we started, only to arrive back at the 'beginning' where the gold had been the entire time.

Yet we'd never have been able to see it with yesterday's eyes.

This is the true power and value of shifting and evolving your perspective. Finding the gold you already had and remembering who you really are.

Re-membering is putting back together, a realizing – or 'making real' your Divinity. It's a process of understanding that you are Source

Energy, choosing to see the world through its infinite, yet one-of-a-kind perspectives – Yours.

Each time you find yourself stopping an old habit of unconstructive self-criticism or catching yourself having a viewpoint that isn't aligned with your highest loving vibration, I want you to reinforce that positive perspective shift.

CALL TO ACTION:

I want you to anchor in that perspective shift by saying out loud, "Perspective Shift! I love you!" It sounds catchier as 'P.S. I love you!'

You're also gifting yourself with the affirmation that you are capable of transforming anything you put your mind, heart, and spirit into, wrapped in a bow of self-love.

Accomplishing just one of these 7 principles, let alone all of them, in the time and space appropriate for you, will – like your new perspectives – shift and evolve your life.

It's a journey, a process, and an endless evolution.

You're finding yourself reading these words for a reason. You're manifesting what you need for unlocking your own PowerPerspective Pathway.

And I wish you all the love and encouragement possible to light your way down the path.

P.S. I LOVE YOU!

Nicole Lite

Divine Intuitive Energy Healer

https://www.linkedin.com/in/nicole-lite-44028226/
https://www.facebook.com/nicole.lite
https://www.instagram.com/soulkisses222/

Nicole Lite is a two-time Cancer Thriver and Stem Cell Transplant recipient, a Divine Intuitive Energy Healer and Reiki Master of over six years and a Spiritual Empowerment Mentor. Her focus is serving both men and women who desire help in moving through obstacles and personal transformations with her combined use of energy healing modalities or with her spiritual guidance.

Nicole writes to share about her personal and spiritual journey during her illnesses which served as a major catalyst in deepening her faith and trust in God and the divine to help guide her through one of the most frightening and challenging times in her life. She shares the many revelations she had while also heavily utilizing her intuition and spirituality to give her the strength she needed to continue on her healing path. She hopes her story will inspire others to keep moving forward through life's challenges, knowing how powerful and resilient they are.

The Healing Rose

By Nicole Lite

Challenges are, unfortunately, a necessary part of this human journey. I'd experienced so many ups and downs and had already tackled so many hurdles in my life, but nothing could have prepared me for these past several years. I do believe, though, that everything that happens to us is part of a divine plan and that every obstacle we encounter is meant to help strengthen us or to lead us down the path that is, ultimately, for our best and highest good. It's only in hindsight that we can try to understand why all these events played out the way they did.

So, here we go. Here's my backstory, and I truly promise you, it'll give you a deeper understanding if you have the whole picture.

In September 2021, I was working in New York City as a legal assistant for a law firm after the pandemic hit, when I was subsequently fired from the firm for refusing to take the COVID-19 vaccine. I was a woman with a very strong love for spiritual development, and a couple of years before I was let go from my job, I learned about the power of Reiki healing and felt a deeper calling to learn it, so I could help heal my family, myself and others, and I became a Reiki Master. So, when I was let go, I took this as a major sign from the universe that it was time for my completely destroyed nervous system to leave corporate America and use my passion for healing to become a spiritual entrepreneur and begin practicing Reiki professionally and to continue my ongoing quest in spiritual development.

If only I had understood what the consequences would be to the life-altering decisions I made or if I had loved and accepted my body as I was, maybe I wouldn't have had to go through this entire chapter. I wasn't happy with what I had and didn't feel as feminine as I could have because my breasts were small, and the density of them had diminished after having my son. But then again, even if it's a hard pill to swallow, everything really does happen for a reason. God does have a plan in all He does.

So, about eleven years ago, I had undergone breast augmentation. I gifted myself this birthday present at the age of forty. I didn't even do this with the intention of pleasing my husband. He actually always told me that he thought I looked perfect the way I was. He truly loved and accepted me in all ways, which is why I always knew when I met him that he would make the perfect husband for me. He was also my best friend and became living proof to me throughout our marriage, how God really always had my back for blessing me with him, the father of our amazing son, and my soul partner.

One day, while going through my Instagram, I stumbled upon a post. I hadn't been feeling well for some time. Extreme fatigue, enlarged lymph nodes, hair loss, joint pain, a rash on my chest, and night sweats, were just some of the symptoms I was experiencing. This Instagram post gave me one nice slap in the face when it started speaking about the topic of Breast Implant Illness. I just knew at that very moment that I was supposed to see it and that it was all in divine timing. It was also the exact catalyst for everything that happened to me from that moment forward.

I started interviewing plastic surgeons who could remove my breast implants immediately. I found my surgeon and had my routine mammogram to prepare me for surgery, only to find out that I had three lumps in my left breast, revealing I had breast cancer and lymphoma simultaneously. I don't know how you'd respond to this, but hearing I had two cancers, let alone one, was the most surreal experience of my life, or at least up until that point. It was an out-of-body experience as if someone was speaking a completely foreign language to me. It was extremely difficult to process it all. I was then advised to first address my breast cancer, and I underwent a double mastectomy without any reconstruction. Since the implants were what made me ill in the first place, my options were limited, and I chose to remain flat for the time being. Quite frankly, reconstruction of any kind at that point in time was not even on my radar and was completely secondary to the fact that I still had a long road ahead of me. The priority was beginning chemotherapy treatment to battle my lymphoma. I need to be real and mention that I had procrastinated for many months because I was so frightened of chemotherapy, but after a lot of soul searching, receiving so much love and support from my friends and family, and receiving a lot of guidance from Source, I moved ahead on my chemo journey.

That winter, I had my 50th birthday while doing chemo and was hospitalized for two weeks with pneumonia and RSV, and finished my treatments in April, or so I thought. After taking my family trip to Aruba with my husband and son in July, I was told by my oncologist that the chemotherapy didn't eradicate all the cancer and that I'd have to undergo a Stem Cell Transplant. Let's just say that I went pretty dark. I spent many weeks pondering about my mortality and feeling deeply depressed. I knew I had to allow myself to feel all of the fear, anger, frustration, and resentment for having to continue this awful journey and, once again, coming face-to-face with the idea that I might die. I felt that I was still so young, that I hadn't finished everything I was meant to do on this earth, and that there was a real possibility I could miss out on seeing my son grow further into his adulthood, graduate college, have a family of his own, and be there for him to love and guide him. My son is my heart and one of my greatest blessings. We have a beautiful and special soul bond. With all these thoughts and concerns, however, I did allow myself the space and grace to feel all the feels and then I pulled myself back together and moved forward in this process.

Don't get me wrong, I was scared to holy hell to have this transplant. I sought spiritual support at every opportunity that was given to me. Even up until the day before I went into the hospital, I was asking Spirit if receiving this Stem Cell Transplant was for my best and highest good. I was also extremely blessed that my son was able to be my stem cell donor. The boy I gave life to and had my whole heart was going to give life back to me, and it was so incredibly powerful and beautiful. My transplant occurred on the day after my actual birthday and was literally the biggest gift I could ever receive from God. I was now going to have my son's DNA and eventually have his blood type, which just blew my mind. This entire chapter was so surreal for me and still hard for me to wrap my head around at times. I will say that my relationship with my son is nothing I take for granted, and I recognize how deeply blessed I am that he chose me to be his mother. He never gave a second thought to being my donor, and I'll forever remind him how special he is to have saved my life.

Now, I'm nine months post-transplant and see everything in hindsight. What I do see is that I moved through this entire cancer journey with as much strength and perseverance as I could. I found so much solace in my connection with Source, my family, my soul sisters, and most importantly, with God. I knew every single interaction I had, every message I received, every doctor who took care of me, every energy healing session I received, and every spiritual and gifted sister who guided me, were all put onto my path to help me along this entire journey. Absolutely everything was divinely orchestrated for me.

I learned what grace, compassion, forgiveness, love, and acceptance look like, and this continues. I learned that the most important relationship of all that needs to be honored and nurtured is the one with yourself. I'd previously held onto so much anger, sadness, grief, frustration, fear, and lack of self-love and acceptance in my body. So much so that I believe whole-heartedly that this is partly why I got sick in the first place. My breast implants also had a major part in poisoning my body. I've made it a mission in my life to heal my mind, body, and soul, which has been the most important healing journey of my existence. I had to let go of a lot of poisonous resentment I had towards certain family members and some other relationships. I had to stop placing expectations on people and come to the true understanding that people can only meet you where they're at and can only extend as much love to you as they are capable of loving themselves. Everyone has their own traumas and fears and acts out of their own pain. You need to extend love, compassion, and understanding to those people, or try your very best. One thing is certain, though; you have to be your own biggest source of love. I started to love myself more, listen, nurture, and support my inner child, and heal the parts of me that ever led me to believe that I was unworthy of receiving love in all its forms.

Learning to love my body was absolutely another facet of healing and self-love that I needed to embrace, especially after going from being a woman who had elective breast augmentation to a woman who had no boobs at all. After my double mastectomy, I emotionally went from not caring about receiving any reconstruction, to feeling incredibly insecure and self-conscious about being flat a year later. Once I underwent my Stem Cell Transplant, I once again completely tabled any concern I had over being flat. To sum it up, my desire to have some type of reconstruction has changed many times over. In the beginning, I felt like I needed to be a martyr and just accept being flat and be at peace with it, and at some point, that feeling changed. I then felt some degree of shame and guilt for desiring to feel more embodied in my femininity by contemplating the possibility of reconstruction, like a DIEP flap procedure, which is a fat transfer from your belly. To be completely honest, I'm still quite uncertain as to how I wish to look, and I'm going to take my time deciding on this one. I do know my feminine essence can never be truly lost. I'll have to see as time goes on how I'd like to physically embody my womanhood. And if I change my mind ten more times, I'll just extend to myself more love and compassion. I'm only human.

This chapter of my life has fundamentally changed and molded me into the version that I am today. If it wasn't for this cancer journey, I know I wouldn't profoundly see every single day, no matter what it brings me, as a gift from God. Every single day gives me an opportunity to learn, grow, experience, and feel. My relationship with God became more intimate. There were many times along this road that had me questioning why and what the purpose of all of this was. With every delay I experienced, He pushed me to trust in Him, surrender my fear and worry, and lay it all at His feet. As you can imagine, when your life's on the line, surrender is so difficult. I became stronger because I knew His word was sound and true.

Several months after my transplant, my oncologist told me that I needed to have a biopsy because they saw something that needed further investigation. The former version of me would have been a crazed lunatic with worry, but this newer version of me was calm and collected. What God did for me on the day of the biopsy, I will never forget. I had prayed to Him that the test would come back benign, but He did one better. As I lay there on the table, ready for the sonogram, both the technician and the doctor found nothing at all to test. I know with every fiber of my being that this happened because I had faith in a positive outcome, and I fully surrendered all to God.

During this period of time, I heavily used my connection to Source, the Angels, my spirit guides, my mother who had transitioned, and my intuition. I had the support and love from my family and soul sisters and I did a lot of deep emotional healing and energy work. I know without a doubt that if I didn't consistently have all of these souls and tools to help guide and give me the strength and courage to keep moving forward, I wouldn't have made it through. I received many signs helping me throughout, and it helped me make some very important decisions. Your intuition is one of the greatest gifts.

Knowing that God, the Angels, my guides, and my mother were with me during this entire chapter, gave me the strength I needed. I also had many energy healing sessions that helped me on an energetic and emotional level. I came to understand more intimately how much trauma and pain are stored in your body and how it deeply impacted my own health negatively. I made it my mission to heal, love, and forgive myself and others and remove any energetic attachments and pain that no longer served me. It's also now one of my greatest passions in my own work as an intuitive energy healer. I know that I'm here to serve humanity by helping to release pain in others, so it doesn't manifest as illness for them in the future.

This chapter illuminated so many aspects of my life. It revealed how I wasn't showing up in the world, how I was dimming my light, not using my voice, and allowing fear to take the front seat. I came to truly understand that time is not something you can ever get back and I wasn't living my life to my fullest potential. Prior to my illnesses, I was living in suppression, afraid to be seen, afraid to speak my truth or share an opinion, and always worried about how my words would be received. I was so afraid of saying something that would run the risk of being judged, unaccepted, or abandoned. This journey continues because I'm still being shown all the ways in which I had previously limited myself.

I never set goals or allowed myself to have desires. I know this came from my upbringing. This is an ongoing journey for me, which is also heavily connected to self-love, acceptance, worthiness, and healing parts of my inner child. I was brought up in a family where my twin sister and I were taught to accept mediocrity, that we should be happy with bare necessities, and that desires were unimportant. What this did was inadvertently teach us that we were not worthy of having more and that desiring luxuries made us greedy. Shame and ridicule were placed on us, and desire was shut down at a very early age. Where is the magic in life if there is no desire? If it wasn't for this deeply emotional aspect of my cancer journey, I don't believe that I would have recognized so clearly how desire was buried so deeply.

I do know I was healed by God for a greater purpose; of course, for myself, for my late mother and maternal lineage, but also to inspire others to heal themselves so that they can live their fullest, most empowered, abundant, and joy-filled lives. I now live my life in a way that I graciously accept every single day, no matter what the day brings. I take each day as a gift; one to learn more about who I am underneath all the layers of societal conditioning and pain from past experiences. Each and every day gives me one more opportunity to grow, to be pushed outside of my comfort zone so I can expand, and to experience the fullness of being a soul in a human body.

I've also learned to love and accept my body no matter what it looks like. Having no breasts and having gained weight since my Stem Cell Transplant, have played a large role in how I feel about my appearance. Accepting that this body is my sacred vessel, how it allows me to be here on earth, and how it will continue to physically change as time moves on, has brought my soul peace and acceptance. I had struggled with embodying my femininity because of the importance I had placed on my appearance, but now I know that your feminine essence can never be taken from you, and it resides in the core of your soul.

It's so important to me that you understand that I see that my cancers were the catalyst I needed in order for me to see many facets in my life that needed healing so I can live my life more intentionally and become everything I'm meant to be. This cancer journey was hardly ever about the physical illness, and all about my divine homecoming and discovering the magic that resides within and with life itself.

Hannah Darby, GMBPsP, SMACCPH

Healing with Hannah
Healer

https://www.linkedin.com/in/hannahdarbyhealingwithhannah
https://www.facebook.com/hannahsdarby
https://www.instagram.com/healingwithhannahd/
https://www.healingwithhannah.co.uk/
https://www.accph.org.uk/martley/therapists-and-coaches/hannah-darby

Hannah has defied childhood bullying and the effects of the death of her Dad in her early teens. She lives with chronic illnesses; re-learning who she is everyday, she didn't even let breaking her back in a serious car accident stop her.

Hannah is a General member of the British Psychological Society, a Senior Member of Accredited Counsellors, Coaches, Psychotherapists and Hypnotherapists, a Reiki Master, HeartHealing™ Practitioner, Crystal lover, Author and Healer.

She runs Healing with Hannah, using her unique blend of professional and personal wisdom to help you recover from grief in your life. She helps you re-discover yourself while living with grief. Let her be your healing guide.

Hannah resides in the British Countryside with her 2 dogs, 4 cats and husband. She's a lover of nature, heavy metal and horror movies, a believer in God and on a lifelong spiritual healing path. She's a woman who defies.

Be the Hero of Your Story

By Hannah Darby, GMBPsP, SMACCPH

I have been defying the odds since I took my first breath. Why? Because I was born blue. I was too excited by life and started breathing too early, filling my lungs with fluid. Luckily, I was whisked away and incubated until I was pink, then placed in the arms of my loving parents. I am so lucky to have been given the opportunity of life, and I grabbed it with both tiny hands. Since then, I have continued to be a woman who defies throughout my life, turning my challenges into advantages.

Life throws curve balls in our direction and places obstacles in our path to help us grow, learn, and become the best version of ourselves we can possibly be. We often don't see it like that at the time, though. I have had a fair few of these in my 37 years on this earth; I am a woman who defies the odds.

I have always seen the world differently to most; this is my gift and my curse. I was severely bullied all the way through my education, always excluded by my peers, making me feel unworthy, rejected, alone, and crushing all my self-esteem. I was a quiet kid, an easy target, plus I loved learning, which was not cool! This left me feeling like an outcast, rejected, and like I didn't belong anywhere. It's when the little voice in my head started to turn negative when my intrusive thoughts placed their first negative seeds. This has impacted my adult life massively, making it hard for me to be visible, not speaking up with my true authentic voice, and generally shrinking into the background, until now. It left me people pleasing, feeling like I was worthless and living in my own constant cloud of doom.

Let me take you back to one particular event that scarred my soul. I had just started high school. I had a group of 'friends' from primary school, well, I thought they were my friends, but in hindsight, most definitely not. One lunchtime, they threw me around the playground on my rucksack, then hung me to the fence high enough I couldn't get down myself. The whole school was there watching and laughing, so I put on a brave face and laughed with them. Eventually, someone took pity on me and unhooked me, I ran to the toilets and cried. This public humiliation left me with deep emotional scarring. I wanted to turn invisible, and this feeling stayed with me until I healed my heart.

I never let them see the pain and hurt they caused. I am so glad I managed to keep my dignity and never showed them the pain they caused. I see now they were never really my friends, I was an object they could use to amuse themselves, until they got bored and found someone else to 'play' with. I am so glad I found out how fake people can be at such an early time in my life. That is one of the greatest lessons I have learnt, and I am the opposite, as I always wear my heart on my sleeve with pride. Life is too short to be wearing masks all the time, and it takes far more energy to be fake than it does to be real. So, my advice is to be your real self. It is not important what anyone else thinks of you, just what you think of yourself.

After another year or so, then the real dark night of my soul arrived, the sudden unexpected death of my father, who was only 50 years old. We were at our grandparents for the weekend, which was not uncommon for us. I was making tea and coffee for us all, I walked into the lounge, and there he was, having a heart attack on the sofa. I froze and shouted for help, we called an ambulance. I was talking to the call handler whilst Mum performed CPR until the ambulance arrived, and we were then shipped off to a neighbour. I always resented this as I wanted to know what was happening, children are capable of handling much more than adults give them credit for. However, I am so glad that I was given the opportunity to say goodbye at the funeral home, giving me some closure. This rocked my world, questioned my faith, and sent me off the rails on a self-destructive cycle. How could a loving God do something like this? What had I done to deserve losing my dad at an age where I felt I was only just really learning who he was?

Grief is a funny thing. It comes and goes in eternal waves—grief is a cycle you keep going around and around, but I tell you, it does not get any easier with time, it just gets more familiar and becomes a part of who you are, part of your identity. Learning how to live my life in grief has been one of my hardest life lessons, but one I feel lucky to have started at such a young age, giving me a true insight into the meaning of life and why we are here. I have seen grief tear people apart and am so grateful I was given this lesson at an age where I was able to learn and grow with it. Grief changes you, not for better or worse, you just become a different version of yourself.

Learning that we cannot control everything in our lives is an important life lesson to learn, but one we find hard as it is in our human nature to try to control ourselves, others, and the world around us. But that perfectionism and control can start to destroy us if we become too hyper-focused on it.

I have always been a control freak, especially around food. I am a sick person, I must have thrown up 1000s of times, if not more, to the point it really doesn't bother me anymore. Honestly, we couldn't make it 3 miles from the house before I got travel sick, and we all had spare clothes in the boot! I have always had severe IBS, food intolerances, and travel sickness, being generally weak in the stomach. This made me have an unhealthy relationship with food. I wouldn't eat anything that was mixed together, I needed to know exactly what I was eating. I was a teenager who had never eaten pizza! Crazy, right? Losing my dad helped me eat better. Wait, work with me here. I realized that some things in life will happen that we have no control over, we have no choice in some things we experience. But, what we can control is our thoughts and feelings, how we want the world to perceive us, and how we let those experiences affect us. I chose to let go of that need to be in control, allowing me to grow a healthier relationship with food.

A shining light of my car accident was that I was referred to the dietician in the hospital as my weight dropped below 6 stone. They introduced me to a low FODMAP diet which has changed my world dramatically for the better. If you suffer from IBS, I urge you to research this, it has been a complete gamer-changer to my relationship with food. I am now a low FODMAP diet pro, so reach out to me if you need any advice, I'm here to help.

Also, a word of advice: I have spent my whole life trying to put on weight and failing. It hurts me deeply when people mention how slim I am, and how I am so lucky to be so small. Well, no!!! I would rather have a bit of healthy extra weight than suffer a lifetime of gut issues. So, be careful with your words, after all, they are mightier than the sword. And what you wish for may not be the shiny happy place you think it is!

So, how did I get through all of these dark nights of the soul? Firstly, find your tribe, like-minded people who accept you for who you are, as you are, dents and all. For me, I found some of this within the Metal music community, they made me feel welcome with open arms, and they were always non-judgemental and so supportive. I found comfort in the lyrics of their songs, knowing there were other people out there feeling the pain I was in. To feel and experience their pain through their music allowed me to express the pain I was in, I finally had found someone who understood me. I finally found a way to release some of my emotions. Listening to their songs made me feel so much less alone.

Secondly, don't try to bury or ignore your thoughts and feelings. Burying them down does you no good at all, they ALWAYS come back with vengeance ten times fold. I tried to numb myself in my teenage years with alcohol and other things, none of which were helpful, constructive or healthy. All to try to make me forget the pain I was in, to try to forget about the hurt and sorrow caused by decades of bullying and the sea of grief I was drowning in after losing my dad. Safe to say, this did not help but made things worse, it fueled the depression in my mind and fanned the anxiety in my body. I turned to self-harm, as this gave me a feeling of control back and made me feel something instead of the emptiness I had inside. I even contemplated suicide. I see these scars every day, and they remind me of how far I have come, how much I have faced, and how I have defied the cards handed to me. It reminds me that one of life's greatest gifts is the depth of our emotions, you can't have the good without the bad, the light without the dark, pleasure without pain. Life is about finding a balance between these opposing forces, building your own ying-yang.

I went on to study Psychology at A-level and at Degree level to try to understand myself better: why I felt the way I did and how my development shaped my mindset. This enabled me to feel less of a freak as I finally understood exactly why and how I felt and reacted the way I did. But I still couldn't change those negative thoughts and feelings, but at least, I knew where they came from and why I had them.

Leaving the country and going on a gap year before university also partly saved my life. I knew if I stayed where I was, my self-destructive mission would end badly. So at 18, I put myself outside my comfort zone and travelled alone to New Zealand, where I worked on a visa for a year. I discovered so much about myself during this time, this was really worth far more than anything else I experienced. I found it easier to talk to people, and even crazier, they were nice to me! It opened my eyes again to the beauty of creation, gave me hope for my life again, and showed me I was worthy, I was wanted, and I was enough as I am. I feel so blessed and grateful to have been given that opportunity.

My husband and I have faced more challenges together than most people do in their lifetimes, but it has made us so much stronger together, and I know that whatever happens, he always has my back.

Going forward a decade or so, my husband and I had just bought our first home together. This should have been an exciting time for us. We moved in just before Christmas, and 1 week later, I had a life-changing car accident. The first week in January, I completely smashed up my T7 vertebrae, I had broken my spine! It was these same vertebrae, when broken, that paralyzed Christopher Reeve (Superman). I spent 1 month in the hospital, unable to move: I had to stay still on the bed, I couldn't even sit up to eat. Let me tell you, eating lying down is a hard thing to do, and using a bedpan will take away any last embarrassing thoughts about yourself you have. Then, when I was finally released, I had to spend 6 months in a back brace, which had to be on any time I was upright. This was one of the most uncomfortable things I have ever had to wear. Even worse, if I had not contacted the hospital, I would still be in it today, as they forgot about me and lost my records. Worcester thought I was under Coventry's care, and Coventry thought I was under Worcester's care! If I hadn't had the sense to contact them and question my care, I would be a lot worse off than I am today. So have the courage to speak up and don't just take things at face value.

But I have never had such a sense of peace, clarity, and a connection to the Divine as I did in those moments before I blacked out. I knew the car was going out of my control, so I relaxed, and said a prayer, "What will be will be, please watch over me, Lord." Then a feeling of calm, oneness with the world, and peace came over me for what felt like an age. Finally, I was turned upside down and ended up facing the wrong way on the other side of the road. I am so pleased I was the only one in the car, as the passenger side came off much worse than the driver's side.

This accident has left me with lasting injuries, a life lived in pain. I had scoliosis, where my muscles healed at different rates bending my spine, I have a wedge where the vertebrae healed funny, meaning I always have to keep pulling my shoulders back, and chronic nerve pain at the break site. Medication and physiotherapy have been a part of my life ever since.

The one thing that has given me the biggest difference in my pain levels is thinking of pain as my old friend. Once I stopped fighting the pain and worked with it instead, it shouted much quieter. I now think I would feel lost without my old friend pain talking in my ear all the time.

Some days it does get louder than others, those are the days I realise I have not been working with it but trying to rebel against it, and trust me, pain always wins.

I am thankful for all my life experiences, as they made me the woman I am today—a woman who heals, a woman who defies!

So, my Psychology degree helped me to work out why I felt the way that I did, giving me the tools to understand my mindset. It gave me names and meaning to the emotions I was carrying around—depression, anxiety, PTSD, GAD, OCD. Studying Reiki and becoming a Reiki Master has allowed me to really drop into myself, to truly feel and experience the emotions I had bottled up and suppressed for so many years, and to see clarity in where they came from and why I was feeling them. It brings me a sense of inner peace and calm I have not found anywhere else. HeartHealing™ has allowed me to release those emotions, it allowed me to express all the pain, anger, and sadness I had been holding on to surrounding my dad's death, in a safe environment, one where I did not feel any shame or guilt for feeling that anger. I have really healed so much in the past year, I never realised I could feel so free. It allowed me to connect all the dots in my story so that I could truly start to heal.

If my story brings light and hope to just one of you beautiful souls reading this, then my job here is done!

Now, I hold my head high with the confidence to share my story with you right now. Finally, I am fully stepping into the amazing, awesome woman I was destined to be. This would never have been possible if I hadn't worked on my mindset with my Psychology degree, discovered the healing power of Reiki to raise my frequency, and healed the wounds of my heart with HeartHealing™ to release all the pent-up emotion I had been holding on to, that had been slowly eating my soul. I found both Reiki and HeartHealing™ so transformative myself that I am now fully trained in both modalities, meaning I can share their healing power with you through my business, Healing with Hannah. You, too, can finally be free to shine your light brightly, find your own balance in life between the light and the dark, defying your odds and empowering yourself to take control of your life again, living life to the fullest. Let me help you put yourself back together with gold. So you can not just survive but thrive. You are not broken, just built differently now. This difference gives you a beauty you didn't have before and gives you wisdom and strength.

I would love to connect with you all, so reach out and say "Hi!" In Healing with Hannah, I use my decades of professional and personal wisdom learned from my journey of a bullied outcast child, a teenager lost in self-destructive addictions, and an adult lost in a cloud of doom. To a woman who has turned a life-changing car accident into a positive path change in my life, a woman who has the strength and resilience to live with chronic life-changing conditions, a woman who defies, a woman who wins!

Tomia Minnis

Founder of The Fulfillment Coach

http://thefulfillmentcoachllc.com/

Hello Lovely! My name is Tomia Minnis! Professional transformation & performance coach, author, speaker, and course creator on a mission of helping women just like her! Tenacious women who have experienced feeling incapable as a result of their self-defeating behaviors. Women who have struggled with mental health and self-perception and have difficulties getting out of their own way in life.

What inspires me to be on this journey the most, is that I too am someone who knows all too well what it is like to experience pain in the deepest forms. Pain that cannot be seen by the naked eye and truly shakes you to your core.

I am also a firm believer that we are not given the privilege of making it through our darkest valleys and deepest despair's without a moral obligation of lending a hand to others who need guidance on how to do the same.

For Women Like Me

By Tomia Minnis

Dedication:

To Logan,

Thank you for loving me and supporting me every step of the way as I chase my dreams. You help me to believe in myself and push towards greatness.

I love you more than words can express and look forward to growing old with you.

Love, Mia

* * *

One day, you're going to be so glad that you didn't quit. That you met every "I can't" with an "I can", took one more step when you'd had enough, tried again tomorrow even though you fell down today. One day, you're going to thank the you that stands here now. The one who continued to show up even though things felt hard. The one who dusted themselves off and found a new way of looking at things. One day, you're going to thank the you that was wise enough to remind you that you can do hard things. The evidence is in all the mountains you've climbed, hardships you've overcome, and the fact that you are here now - still standing.

- Salt and Whistle

There have been many chapters in my life where I have begged God to take it all away. Pages that were filled with countless tears, heartache, and debilitating pain.

Paragraphs of negative self-talk, and thoughts on repeat telling me that this life is too much for me to bear.

Sentences of hoping that I could stop feeling anything because feeling nothing was better than drowning in my sorrows.

I thank God every day that my story continues to be one that is continually being written and that he put a comma where more than once in my life, I wanted so badly to put a period.

When The Light First Started To Become Dim:

I have struggled with mental health for most of my life starting at around 11 years of age. I was met with a hardship I never could have expected to endure. This is the same year my mother was diagnosed with cancer. She fought like hell, but It quickly deteriorated her body and took her life less than a year later.

My mother was truly something special. She was the perfect example of standing in your faith in even the hardest times. She taught me to seek the lord in all seasons of life. She was the greatest example of strength. She was a talented writer and an outstanding mom.

I am grateful to have had the time I did with her and the lessons she taught me before her departure still stick with me to this day.

Having a front-row seat to watching cancer deteriorate my mother's body to skin and bones, making her nearly unrecognizable, while also not being able to do a damn thing about it messed me up.

There is something about watching someone suffer and not being able to take the pain away that hits deep in your soul.

I remember a day or so before she passed when my mother was in a medicated coma. In a moment alone, I cried and told her that it was okay to let go so that she no longer had to suffer any longer.

That is a pain that will never not sting. And I miss her today just as much as when she perished, that was 13 years ago now.

Mom, You Are Never Forgotten:

She wasn't just my mother. She was so much more than that.

She was the true embodiment of love.

She was the best friend who stood by my side no matter what.

She's the one who loved me without condition and I wouldn't be half the person I am today if it weren't for her and all she has shown me.

- Jenna Lowthert, The Weight of What's Gone

Grief is ultimately the experience of coping with any type of loss. But, I'd say that when that loss is of someone you hold dear, it truly shakes us to our core.

Grief is widely recognized and understood as a universal emotion that we have all experienced in one way, shape, or form.

In my opinion, there is something so beautiful and wicked about grief. And they tend to coincide with one another.

It's wicked because many of us have experienced some of the toughest thoughts and emotions while experiencing the stages of grief. But beautiful as we grieve those we have lost because of the love and wonderful memories we have shared.

We grieve them in remembrance of what was and also what we wished would be.

Grieving, and sharing stories, tears, and laughs about them quite literally keeps their memory alive.

I struggle with the fact of the matter that my mother was not able to be earth-side with me through both trivial and pivotal moments of my life. She didn't get the opportunity to see me walk at graduation, or send me off to prom. She didn't get to meet the love of my life that I feel she would adore and approve of especially the man he has flourished into. She won't get to physically be there at my wedding, or the birth of her future grandchildren, they won't get to know her personally and experience her ever-encompassing love, compassion, and infectious laugh.

And in all honesty It feels so unfair to not have had the privilege many others have been granted. And frankly, that is the main reason I lost my faith in God at that time in my life as well.

Losing Faith:

I asked God "Why?" an innumerable amount of times. I couldn't understand why this hardship would happen, why she had to go, and why she had to perish in such a painful way.

I took it very personally that my mother was no longer with me while many other friends and classmates still had their parents around.

My adolescent brain could not fathom why such a horrible event had to not only happen to my mother, but to me, and our family as well.

She was oh so loved and adored. The literal glue of our family, and we have not been the same since her passing.

So for several years, I didn't speak to God. I avoided church. I honestly wanted absolutely nothing to do with him. I was angry with God and I did not know how to best handle that anger. At this point in my life, I did not understand that I could cast my hurts and worries upon him as he cares for me. (1 Peter 5:7)

Without Jesus in my life, my life was hell after my mother passed. I experienced more hardships and traumas. I trusted, encountered, and gave my love to people I in hindsight wish I never had.

My mental health continued to plummet and snowball, therapy, and medication were not helping in the long term.

Without Jesus, my life was a literal dumpster fire.

Being Free:

What set me free and returned me to Jesus is that I finally realized that those hardships and pains are things that are not for me to understand.

What brought me back to him was a realization of just how broken and lost I had become without his love and guidance.

What brought me back to God especially initially was a desperation for healing and peace I finally recognized only he can provide for me.

Understanding God's plan and purpose for our life is not for us to fathom. We can free ourselves from the chains of our human understanding and lean on the one who has a plan and purpose for our lives. (Jeremiah 29:11)

So, I may never completely understand why these crushing moments happened in my life. But, I am at a place where I am okay with that.

After all, I know where I am headed and I believe when my time has come and God calls me home, my mother and I will meet again.

Until then, I continue to live my life as much as possible and seek God for guidance and strength.

Continued Struggles:

My mental health issues like many of you never completely subsided. It is something that sticks with me and tends to intensify and show its face at some of the worst times. Kind of like those damn car troubles you never see coming or unexpected expenses you did not plan for.

This past year for me is an example of that. I started 2024 doing very well, taking care of my mind, body, and spirit. I was heavily focusing on my future and business goals and making progress. I even took the leap and invested a decent chunk of change in improving my business and speaking knowledge.

And in an instant, I took a step forward, and the ground crumbled at my feet. Within what felt like seconds, I was isolating, having very negative thoughts, and quickly couldn't care less if I lived or died.

In hindsight, I recognize that it was in the moments of silence alone without any distraction that the pains I had been avoiding for so long had the prime opportunity to bubble to the surface.

That's the thing about distraction. It can most definitely be a way to cope with difficult situations and feelings. But just like many other things, when we overindulge it has the potential to become detrimental to our lives.

I have had several mental health fallouts. Including a full-blown psychosis mania. So spiraling downward and at a rapid pace was not something I was not familiar with. This year hands down takes the cake.

I am thankful to God that I continued to fight and mustered the courage to research and reach out for the help I desperately needed. As a result of getting said help, I received some diagnoses that were bittersweet but assisted me in understanding myself better. And completed multiple mental health programs that have had a lasting effect on my life and taught me so very much about myself, coping skills, crisis signs, and lots more.

In fact, I am currently in another program once a week as I am writing this.

This year, I fought like hell and vowed to give myself the opportunity to heal and thrive in this life. I no longer wished to keep avoiding and distracting myself from things that were affecting my everyday life and causing me to not see myself as worth it.

I inform you of these deeply personal things to show you that mental health is not something to hide from or be embarrassed by. It's not something to wish away. It's not something to play with either. It is something to acknowledge. It is something to work through. It is something to reach out for help when and if it is needed.

Don't get me wrong, I know all too well that mental health is something that is not for the faint of heart. When we are in the thickest and darkest parts of the woods of our minds, we do not see a way out or a point in reaching out for help, we may even feel like a burden or that those around us do not care, and this is when we need help the most.

Mental health is heinous and can cause us to believe things that were never true. But we find false evidence to believe our accusations.

It can make us believe that we are not worth fighting for, we aren't loved, we aren't worth the time of day, we will never heal, we are incapable of love. The list goes on as far as the eye can see.

Healing:

So yes, this year has been hell, but I am stronger for it. Getting the help I need has taught me so much about myself, it has shown me that I am not alone and that plenty of other people have the same feelings and struggles we may have even though our experiences or demographics are completely polar opposites.

This past year I have met some amazing people that I am honored to have even had a smidge of impact on their mental health journey. People who saw me on some of my darkest days accepted me and understood me. People I will hold dear to my heart for the rest of my days.

Focusing on my mental health for the last several months has been quite a journey. One I have finally accepted I will be on for the rest of my life. One I have finally accepted is not linear and that that is completely normal.

I no longer wish to hold on to false narratives that life is consistently supposed to be peaches and rainbows. Life is well, life. There will be struggle, there will be pain, there will be hardship, there will be troubled times. And there will also be joy, laughter, and beautiful moments that remind us why it is all worth it.

Truthfully, working on letting go of that false expectation that life is not supposed to ever be hard or have pain has also helped me in moving forward and accepting life for what it is.

Life is a crazy rollercoaster of ups and downs that we need to have to appreciate the highs.

I truly believe that hardship can be a real teacher. It teaches us strength, resilience, and wisdom. It builds character, mental muscle, and tenacity. In my own experience, I have not been able to learn and experience these teachings when life is going just as planned.

So I try my damnedest to embrace what life throws at me. Not take it so personally and try to shift perspective from "Woe as me" to "What is this trying to teach me.", "What can I or did I learn from this experience."

Working on your mental health, to say the least, is a lot of work. It takes time, support, effort, and accountability both external and internal. There will be days where you feel on top of the world and there will be days where things start to feel like they are falling apart.

But it has been one of the most rewarding journeys I have ever embarked on.

You Are Not Alone:

I want you to know that If you aren't ready or able to take that step towards healing yet, please know that I and many others completely understand. Hell, I was just in your shoes before the summer.

It is incredibly hard to acknowledge and accept that something may be wrong and for most of us, even more difficult to accept and reach out for help. Society has a way of portraying that needing and asking for help is a weakness. When in reality it is one of the true embodiments of strength.

I want you to know that there are so many people who love you, who understand you, and want to help you.

You are not a burden and the ones who care about you deeply want to see you genuinely smile and not the mask we who deal with mental health become accustomed to wearing.

My hope and prayer for you is to someday see the beauty that is within the ashes. The beauty that lies within even some of the darkest parts of who you are.

I hope that you one day will see that we all struggle and have experienced pain and stop comparing yourself to others.

I hope that you see this life as something truly worth fighting for and that you get to a point where you dig your heels in and do the work that you need and only you can do to change your circumstances.

I hope that you incorporate God in your healing journey. Stop asking "Why", and start asking God for healing, guidance, strength, and love.

Send Off:

Life can bring some of the deepest pains and hardest trials you could have never seen coming. Likely hitting you out of nowhere like a freight train. But what we gain from rising out of the darkness and sometimes even crawling to see the light, we could never gain from the days that are filled with rainbows and not a care in the world.

So yes, like many of you, I have not been dealt the best hand of cards. But I refuse to stop fighting. I refuse to not learn from my trials and learn the lessons I needed to learn, to build the strength, resilience, wisdom, and character that make up who I am.

I also am working on making it a point to appreciate the days in my life when there are pretty blue skies with no rain in the forecast. To stop waiting for the other shoe to drop, and realize that it's going to eventually so why not take in the scenery and laugh until your belly hurts anyway?

Pain has a heinous way of making us feel like we are alone and the only person on this earth who has ever been through a similar experience or shared some of the same thoughts, feelings, and emotions.

And sure, I know someone else has not walked every single step you have in your life. But I can assure you someone out there understands what you are feeling, has had the same thoughts, and experienced the same emotions.

For the love of all things holy, please do not let this false ideation keep you from speaking up, seeking community, and getting the help you need.

Needing and asking for help will never equal weakness. It is the greatest embodiment of strength.

Sending love, prayers, and the biggest hug your way.

And with that, I will leave you with this:

My scars remind me that I did indeed survive my deepest wounds. That in itself is an accomplishment. And they bring to mind something else, too. They remind me that the damage life has inflicted on me has, in many places, left me stronger and more resilient. What hurt me in the past has actually made me better equipped to face the present.

— Steve Goodier

Emily Whitacre

Unboxed Grace Counseling
Co-Founder & Therapist

https://www.linkedin.com/in/emily-whitacre-1a542a22a/
https://www.facebook.com/profile.php?id=100095262228437
https://www.instagram.com/unboxedgracecounseling/
https://www.unboxedgracecounseling.com/
https://www.unboxedgracecoaching.com

Emily Whitacre, LMHCA is a passionate mental health advocate, therapist & coach, co-founder of Unboxed Grace Counseling, and a devoted mom and wife. Alongside her husband and two children, she finds peace and joy in the great outdoors, especially near water or along sandy shores. At Unboxed Grace Counseling, located in Ft. Wayne, IN, Emily is committed to providing compassionate, faith-inspired mental health services for her community. Her personal journey as a mother to a young kidney transplant recipient has instilled a profound empathy, particularly for parents of children with disabilities, and her work is especially dedicated to supporting women and moms, recognizing the unique challenges they face. She blends her love of service with her personal experience and clinical expertise to create safe, nurturing spaces for those seeking hope and healing, in the counseling room and out.

Making a Message Out of a Mess

By Emily Whitacre

The 'wounded healer archetype' is a term coined by psychiatrist Carl Jung, who was a pioneer in analytical psychology. Jung's theory on personality development included the wounded healer, along with eleven other archetypes that make up the foundation of human personality. According to Jung, a wounded healer is someone who uses their own pain and experience with struggle and hardship to help others.

By the time I was 23 years old, I had already navigated more than my fair share of crises. I was the poster child for a wounded healer candidate and started to realize that I had zero control over my life, even though control was what I had been desperately trying to keep for years. Though my outer world looked okay—I had graduated college with honors and had a full-time job that I thought was leading to a great career—my inner world was a mess, and it was threatening the stability of my circumstances.

The Beginning of Surrender

Fed up with how my life was going, and after some wise counsel from my dad, who had always been my guide in life, I opened my heart and mind to a new idea: letting go. Having grown up a Christian, I always had this thought in the back of my head that everything happens for a reason, but I had never put much stock into what that meant in my life. Quite frankly, the thought had brought me nothing but anger for a long time because it constantly made me feel like I was being punished for "not being a good enough Christian." "Everything happens for a reason" meant that I was the reason that things weren't going well in my life, even though I wanted to be "good."

So, I gave up.

I know, it's not quite the heroic mindset you'd expect, given the chapter's title. But what good is sharing a joyous and victorious story without also sharing the raw and vulnerable struggle to get there? So, when I say I let go, what I mean in this context is *I gave up*. I don't think it was quite the approach my dad meant, but I've always had a knack for doing things my own way.

When I gave up and let go, I also truly prayed for the first time in a long time, even though I was so angry at God, and He did something extraordinary, again. Now, one of my favorite scripture verses is Romans 8:28, "And we know that in all things God works for the good of those who love him, who have been called according to his purpose" (NIV). Even when I stopped working then, God didn't.

Identity, Purpose, and Plan

At about the same time I was having this identity, mindset, and purpose crisis, I also had a major career shift. I moved back from my college town, started a new job in a more rehabilitative role as a behavioral technician working with adolescents, and did some intense Biblical soul-searching. The kind of searching that fills notebook after notebook with tear-stained prayers, confessions, and vulnerable hopes for the future. Pages filled with words and thoughts about my identity that came from God and His Word, not what my pain and shame said about me.

And I began to heal. I began to believe the words I was writing on the page.

When I gave up trying so hard to fit the image and expectation I had created, it allowed a new image to start to form: a beautiful image of a girl radiating with love for others, herself, and God. An image that could see a future other than the lonely, isolated existence I was currently living was painting. This idea of thinking in a new way isn't just the biblical concept of "renewing your mind" that is described in the book of

Romans, chapter 12. In my line of work, we call this perspective-taking, or cognitive restructuring. Scientifically this is referred to as neural plasticity, or the ability to rewire the brain through growth and reorganization. I was healing from the inside out.

If you don't believe in coincidence, then it won't be shocking to learn that about the time this healing began, I met the man who would later become my husband. In fact, it was about a month after I moved back to Fort Wayne, and had 'given up' on finding a relationship, that I met Kevin. I would love to say that this is where my story ended, that I was fully healed, that we got married, had our children, and we were living happily ever after. In many ways, we truly are living happily ever after because that is how we choose to view it; however, the healing that I had just begun would become more important than ever, because God was still working in my life.

After about a year together, Kevin and I began making plans for our future, and I began to dream again about my career and what I wanted it to look like, having settled into my new position after a recent promotion. My soul-searching activities had become full-fledged spiritual disciplines, and my own healing experience had come to the point of inspiring me to think about counseling others, to make a message out of my mess. I was thrilled when I was accepted early into a graduate counselor education program, and I was terrified when a month later, I found out we were pregnant.

Though it wasn't a total surprise at the time, I was scared because I had decided early in my adulthood that I was not going to have kids. I was career-focused, and just not cut out for parenting. We'd had a conversation about it and decided that IF it happened, a baby would be welcome, but if I'm being completely honest, I figured that it would just never happen. In fact, I was counting on it. I was counting on God's plan matching mine and His understanding that I was definitely not "mom material."

So yes, I was terrified, because there I was, absolutely pregnant, and absolutely certain I had no idea what I was doing, and that I was going to screw it up. And, oh yes, I was also going to be starting grad school about the same time I was going to be having a newborn.

After about two weeks of pure panic, stress-eating, brutally honest conversations with Kevin, and finally, tearful prayers, I started to feel something else: joy. I knew that making school work with a newborn and a full-time job was going to be super intense. I also knew that my support system was amazing, and I believed in my own academic abilities to carry me through. I was ready. More than ready, I was excited, we were excited.

What we were not ready for was to hear the words "I'm going to go get the doctor" when we went for a routine check-up appointment near the mid-way mark of my pregnancy. The ultrasound tech stopped the imaging no sooner than she began, uttered the words, and added something about making sure the lab nurses didn't leave. She tried her best to be as casual as she could, but it was like a moment from a Lifetime movie. I can remember the room vividly, the smell and the quietness while we waited. The only sound was our breathing, which was growing more rapid and shallower by the minute as I realized that circumstances were dwindling out of my control, again.

The remainder of my first pregnancy was a whirlwind, and somewhat infamous in my little neck of the woods. I was 24 years old and 16 weeks pregnant when I underwent surgery for the first time, so a medical team at Cincinnati Children's Hospital could operate on my unborn child, named Henry, by this point. I'll spare you the confusing medical jargon, but the Cliff Notes version is that Henry had a birth defect called Bladder Outlet Obstruction (BOO, for short, you can Google it), that prevented urine from draining in the uterus, which created a cascading trickle effect that impacted his lung, heart, and kidney development. The surgery was not experimental, but there was also no guarantee it would work. If it did work, we were looking at life-altering and life-long medical complications for our son.

In the span of less than seventy-two hours, I signed not only consent for myself and my unborn son to receive this surgery but also a resignation of employment and a withdrawal from the graduate program I had been accepted into. It might sound dramatic, but in that moment I felt like I was watching my entire future crumble in front of me—again. This time though, I didn't feel hopeless, I couldn't, I had this tiny person depending on my hope and determination to keep moving forward. So, I was letting go, again, but not giving up this time.

One chapter is not nearly enough time to share all of my son's incredible medical journey since that surgery, which was mostly successful. Underdeveloped and damaged kidneys and lungs at birth led to NICU stays at two hospitals for a total of 179 days. Henry was six months old when he came home from the hospital for the first time. The first four years of his life included weekly speech, occupational, and physical therapies, at least monthly visits to the dialysis clinic two hours away, and regular appointments with lung, heart, kidney, eye, and dental specialists. He underwent more than 40 procedures that required anesthesia and received two different kinds of dialysis, which included driving him two hours one-way to the clinic up to five days a week.

Light in the Tunnel

On his 4th birthday, in his 40th-ish surgery, Henry received a kidney transplant from a wildly generous living donor. We celebrated and sang "Happy Birthday" and "Victory in Jesus" as we walked with him to the operating room that day. During these years, while I was no longer employed as a behavioral technician, I was certainly using the skillset, acting as Henry's medical case manager. I was part secretary, part nurse, part therapist, part chauffeur, part Mom, and I still longed to be part helper for others. I heard a small voice inside that grew continuously louder, saying, "Make your mess your message."

Great, I didn't mind sharing, but I didn't know what my message was. So, I threw myself into research and advocacy, offering support and hope whenever I could to other parents in similar situations. I often found myself counseling other moms in waiting rooms, consulting with doctors and therapists about my findings regarding Pediatric Medical Traumatic Stress, or brainstorming about support programs with the nurses and staff on hospital floors that we frequented through the years. I became a social worker, and my first client was my own family.

After Henry received his kidney transplant, which is aptly called the "Gift of Life" in the medical world, we really could begin living. Things that were once impossible—going to school, going on vacation, buying a home, going back to work, having more children—were back on the table. We added our beautiful daughter Gertie to our family shortly after the transplant, and my advocacy work secured the resources Henry needed to live and thrive at home and at school, even through a global pandemic. Instead of coordinating daily or weekly visits with doctors, it slowed to monthly or even yearly visits. But despite any changes, and the control I regained of my life, the voice remained: "Make your mess your message."

The problem was that I didn't feel qualified to share my message with others. There were so many pieces of my story and message that were so vulnerable, raw, and uncontrollable, that I felt *shame* even though there was victory, like I was a fake, an imposter. I became convinced that if I had a bunch of letters after my name, people would be more likely to listen to me, and I told myself that God wanted me to pursue my education again. So, I pulled out my dusty resume, updated it, and sent it back to the same program I had been accepted to seven years earlier, hoping the bits of my story I felt willing to share throughout the application process would be enough to earn me a spot in the competitive cohort. Through a series of related but not-coincidental events, I soon found myself working full-time, going to grad school, and raising a family. Sounds familiar, doesn't it? And I was completely in control of life until I wasn't.

The Slow Climb Up

School got really intense in a number of ways, work got increasingly busy and overwhelming, and then Henry contracted an infection and got really sick. I can distinctly remember one week in which I was living in a hospital room with Henry on one side of town while checking families into the local Ronald McDonald House, where I worked at the hospital on the other side of town. I took Midterms from that hospital room, and left Henry to play games with the nurses, his dad and sister, or family that came to visit while I attended class. Even after he recovered and came home, life was crazy and busy and messy—again—and I was desperately clinging to control.

Letting go of control again was hard. I grieved, stepping away from my position at the Ronald McDonald House. Given my experience with Henry after he was born, I thought for sure it was my dream job that I was supposed to be at forever. I had to realign myself and my thoughts with what I knew to be true, rather than what I felt I wanted. It was difficult, but letting go of that dream let God resurrect one that I had given up on long ago, a dream that I am working toward today, even while writing this chapter of my story.

A decade after applying to graduate school for the first time, I graduated with my master's degree and earned my associate license in mental health counseling in the state of Indiana. I am abundantly blessed to have had the opportunity to co-found a private counseling practice in my community with a dear friend, and I have the honor every day of sitting with people who are working toward their own journey of healing. It is my hope that my own experience of continuously choosing to let go of control, and aligning myself with my values and my identity in Christ, can provide encouragement for others.

Faith in the Formula

When I share my experience over the last decade, people often say, "I don't know how you did it!" and I will semi-jokingly respond: Jesus and coffee. This isn't entirely untrue. My days were—and still are—filled with pretty strict routines that included copious amounts of caffeine and the Word of God, however I could get it. I completed Bible studies, listened to sermons, Christian podcasts, and worship music, and I started having daily conversations with God. Four hours a day in a car with a toddler leaves A LOT of time for self-reflection. For me, these conversations were the same as those tear-filled journal pages of my earlier years, and the process remains true today.

By dwelling on what I know to be true about myself and God, I can let go of the need to control, worry, and fear about my situation, no matter what the circumstances. Where there is chaos and uncertainty, there is also joy and peace. This is how I turned my test into my testimony. It's how this wounded healer helps others learn to make a message out of what seems like a mess.

In the work I do as a mental health counselor, I often tell people that I work with that coming to therapy itself isn't a magical solution that will fix all their problems. There is no one "secret formula" to feel better, but what I can help them with is designing a lifestyle that promotes their own wellness, and it looks a little something like what you've been reading throughout my story.

- **Figure out who you are and what is important to you** - find out what you're rooted in, what drives you, what your values are, and lean into them
- **Let go of what you can't control** - whether you give it to God, the universe, or simply push it out of your focus, dwelling on what you can't control or change only leads to anxiety and stress

- **Find people who are in your corner, and keep them close -** we aren't meant to do life alone. Find the people who support you, who hold you accountable, who enrich your life, and spend it with them!

In life, it's often in the messiest and most uncertain moments that we find the greatest opportunities for growth, healing, and purpose. My story is not one of perfection or complete resolution, but of learning to trust the process of letting go, embracing faith, and finding meaning in the chaos. Each step—whether through heartbreak, fear, or triumph—has been a reminder that our greatest challenges can also become our most profound testimonies. We all carry wounds, but when we lean into them with courage and vulnerability, they can become a source of light, and healing for others. As you navigate your own story, I encourage you to remember this: it's not about controlling every moment, but about embracing who you are, surrendering to what you cannot control, and allowing faith, love, and connection to guide you. Your mess can become your message, and your story has the power to inspire others in ways you may never imagine.

Maureen Denise

CEO of Diva Designs Hair Studio

https://www.linkedin.com/in/dr-maureen-mcdonald-watkins-dpc-chw-cha-66b13559/
https://www.facebook.com/nesi.mcdonaldwatkins/
https://www.instagram.com/nesiisflawless/

Maureen Denise was born January 21, 1967, in South Carolina. With a lifetime of experience as a mother of two and a grandmother of three, a significant challenge in my early years demanded resilience, fueling my determination and discovering talents that would guide my future. My journey eventually led me to beauty and fashion, where my passion flourished. After graduating from beauty school with a focus on hair, I continued my education at the National Institute of Cosmetology, ultimately earning a doctorate in the field. For over 30 years, I owned and operated a salon, using my skills to serve and uplift my community. My love for bringing people together inspired me to host creative events, fostering connection and joy. Now, I hope to share the lessons and accomplishments I've gathered along the way, hoping my story may inspire and support others on their own paths.

Scars of Grace

By Maureen Denise

At sixteen and in 11th grade, I stood at a crossroads, eager to decide my next move. I was immersed in a fashion and merchandising course at the Career Development Center, a place that felt like home. Fashion wasn't just a hobby; it was a passion that pulsed through my veins, and the world of modeling captivated my imagination, filling my thoughts with dreams just waiting to be realized.

In high school, my days were split between classes at the Career Development Center in the mornings and regular classes in the afternoons. Spending half the day away meant missing some of the usual moments with friends, but I never really worried about fitting in. I got along with everyone—boys, girls, even the ones others avoided. One girl, in particular, stood out. We'd grown up together, and she was known for her fiery temper and fighting spirit. She'd been through rough times; you could see it in her shifting moods—anger, sadness, and rare moments of happiness. People often whispered about her family's reputation for stirring up trouble and even ganging up on others.

One afternoon in middle school, on the walk home, things boiled over between us. I wasn't one to start fights; I usually avoided them. But that day, the crowd urged us on, and when she pushed me, something in me snapped. We ended up on the ground, fists flying, while the crowd cheered. Her cousin eventually broke it up, and just like that, it was over. Oddly enough, we drifted back into friendship afterward. That's just how things went back then; no grudge was ever too big to get in the way of being friends.

High school had brought a new mix of faces, but she and I were still cool. We lived on the same street, rode the same bus, and even shared a circle of friends. Everything seemed fine between us. Then, one day, as I was heading back from the Career Development Center, I started hearing rumors—people whispering that there'd be a fight on the bus ride home. To my surprise, the fight was supposed to involve me.

On the bus, the air buzzed with people talking and laughing, as if they were waiting for a show. I wasn't alone that day; a friend of mine was with me after a community club meeting, and we took seats up front. But the talking kept up, and I could only take so much. So, I finally stood up and made my way to the back, where I found her sitting. I asked, "What's the problem? What's going on?"

She shot back, "Get out of my face," and swung her umbrella, catching me on the arm. That was it—I snapped, throwing a few quick punches before the bus pulled up to her stop. I was so caught up in the moment that I wouldn't let her off the bus until someone pulled me aside so she could pass. The bus erupted with cheers and laughter, people even calling me "Sugar Ray Leonard."

I had to laugh, though fighting wasn't really my thing. But if someone hit me first, I was ready to defend myself. Growing up with only sisters, we'd spent plenty of time watching wrestling and boxing on TV, picking up a few moves so we'd know how to handle ourselves.

Deep down, I knew another fight was coming. When I got home, I called one of my sisters, who was away at college. I told her what had happened, and she didn't hesitate. "You know that family likes to double-team people. You've got to be ready," she warned. So, I laid out comfortable clothes and my sneakers, mentally preparing myself for whatever might go down.

The next morning, I was determined to leave yesterday behind. As I walked to the bus stop, the whispers and laughs about the fight still lingered in the air. One guy even joked, "I'm getting on the bus before you. I don't want y'all falling back on me if it starts again." I boarded last, scanning the seats until I saw her, just three rows behind the bus driver. My plan was to ignore yesterday and keep my distance, so I looked away as I passed her. But that was a mistake.

A heartbeat later, everything changed.

The moment her hand connected with my face, I remember the shock—it felt like a slap. Instinct kicked in, and my books hit the floor as my hand shot to her throat, my other hand swinging in defense. Then, someone yelled about a knife. Panic rippled through the bus, and two people lunged to hold her arms, struggling to pry the blade from her grip. I didn't even know I'd been cut until I felt the warm spray of blood from my face. Suddenly, everyone noticed, and someone shouted, "Get her off the bus!"

Dazed, I stumbled down the steps, missing a few as I tried to catch my balance. When I finally stood up, I touched my face and felt the wound, torn wide open. My neighbor, without missing a beat, pressed her white sweater against my face to slow the bleeding—a quick instinct that I marveled at, given we were just sixteen. There was no time to wait for an ambulance. She led me down the street to her house, where her grandfather hurried us to the hospital.

When we arrived, the staff rushed me to the back, working to stem the bleeding. Nurses asked me for information, but I was barely able to think straight. I managed to tell them my mom worked at the hospital, though I knew this news would hit her hard. She knew about yesterday's fight, but when she saw my face wrapped up, she demanded, "Unwrap her."

The nurses did, revealing the open wound. My mom spun around, her voice fierce: "Get the police here now!" But in that moment of chaos, a small blessing appeared—a plastic surgeon happened to be on call that day.

I couldn't believe any of it was real. It felt like I was in some kind of movie. When I woke up from surgery, I saw police stationed outside my hospital door, letting no one in. But somehow, my cousin managed to slip past them. She went to a different high school, so I still don't know how she found out so fast, but there she was, standing by my side.

When it was time to go home, I felt the weakness from all the blood I'd lost. My clothes hung off me, loose and baggy, like I'd shrunk overnight. And as the days went by, the reality of it all started to sink in. I had visitors for weeks, people talking, sympathizing, and sharing their own anger on my behalf. But all that chatter only seemed to fuel my own bitterness. I felt myself growing quieter and angrier, as I turned over and over in my mind what I'd do next. Every time I looked in the mirror, the thought of revenge was right there, burning in me. My dreams of modeling and fashion merchandising felt shattered, fading before I could even grab hold of them. I was numb.

One afternoon, when I was home alone, I stood staring at my reflection, my mind weighed down by the thought of that scar. I felt this strange, intense pressure to take action, to make things right myself. And then, out of nowhere, I heard a soft whisper, like a voice close to my ear, "Let the Lord handle it." It startled me, but I wasn't afraid. I stood there, thinking. If I kept letting anger guide me, I knew I'd probably end up in prison, and all those people around me, pushing me on, would just move on with their lives.

The next day, I looked in the mirror again, staring at that scar, and I made a choice, the hardest choice I'd ever made at sixteen. Looking up, I called out as if He were right there with me, "Okay, Lord, I'm gonna let you handle it."

The moment I made that decision, I felt a shift within me. The weight of the cut faded away, and I found myself living life fully again. My friends, the people I surrounded myself with, treated me as if nothing had ever happened. They filled my days with laughter, constantly assuring me that they couldn't even see the scar.

Strangely enough, I never crossed paths with the girl who had hurt me. We lived in the same city, yet she seemed to vanish from my life for years. I would occasionally hear whispers of her struggles, but the news didn't stir any feelings in me; it was as if I had moved on completely.

A year after high school, I decided to enroll in cosmetology school, another path that kept me in the beauty industry. Life took a wonderful turn when God blessed me with two children. My focus shifted entirely to them, and in caring for their beauty and happiness, I found fulfillment. I turned my passion into a career, enhancing the beauty of others, and eventually, I opened my own business. At this point in my life, I was busier than ever, but it felt right—like I was finally where I was meant to be.

One night, as I was closing my salon with my daughter by my side, I heard a soft knock at the door. When I opened it, my heart dropped—it was the girl who had cut me. I looked at her, my expression questioning, "What do you want?" An unexpected rush of old feelings flooded back, stirring up anger I thought I had left behind. She stood there, her own daughter beside her, and asked if she could come in. Despite my initial hesitation, the God in me felt compelled to let her in.

She began by telling me how heavy the weight of guilt had been on her conscience for the past eight years. I hadn't even realized so much time had passed; God had kept me so busy that I hadn't thought about it. She apologized, explaining that she had finally uncovered the truth—that I had never spoken ill of her. It turned out that people had fabricated lies just to incite conflict between us, leaving her scared for life because of it. "You're still so pretty," she added, and in that moment, something shifted inside me. I felt a wave of compassion for her, recognizing how hard it must have been to carry such guilt for so long and finally find the courage to apologize.

Forgiveness isn't easy, but I knew I had to extend it, especially knowing that I would want God's forgiveness for my own shortcomings. It was a necessary part of moving forward in life. She acknowledged that we might never be friends again but hoped that if we crossed paths in the future, we could simply wave at each other. I replied, "I forgive you, but don't get too comfortable—I might have a flashback." I said that because it was true; we need to keep allowing God to work in our lives. Old feelings can resurface and throw us off balance, and while I felt strong in that moment, I knew I wasn't completely healed.

Years later, I relocated my salon and gave it a new name, focusing on balancing my business and home life. One particular day, while chatting with a client, I shared how I had come to understand God's work in my life, especially regarding the incident of my injury. This client had been coming to me every two weeks, so I was taken aback when, at her next appointment, the girl who had cut me walked through the door.

She approached me and asked if I would do her hair. I paused, taking in her request. After examining her hair, I replied, "You don't need any chemical services; you just need to use the right maintenance products." So, I set to work, applying the products and styling her hair until it looked just right. She complimented me on my own hair and asked how much she owed me. "You don't owe me anything," I said, and she smiled gratefully before leaving.

Turning to my client, I asked, "Do you know who that was?" Her eyes widened in disbelief. "No!" she exclaimed. "That was the girl who cut me," I revealed, and my client was stunned. "I thought you two were friends!" she said. "That wasn't me; that was God," I replied. I felt in my spirit that the girl had come to the salon seeking assurance that I had truly forgiven her.

As time passed, I relocated my salon once more, drawn to better opportunities. One day, I received a call from the daughter of the girl who had hurt me. "Please don't penalize me for what my mom did," she said, her voice trembling. I assured her, "Oh no, I wouldn't do that. I'd be happy to give you a haircut." She made an appointment, and when she arrived, we talked about her struggles. I offered her advice on how to rebuild her life, and to my delight, she took it to heart.

As the months went by, she would visit my salon whenever she was in town, always stopping by for a hug. It struck me how God had guided me to help her, even though I hadn't fully understood why at the time. Now, as I look back and connect the dots, I realize how beautifully woven our stories have become.

As the years passed, I would often cross paths with the girl who had once hurt me—whether it was at the bank or a neighborhood reunion. Strangely, I felt nothing when I saw her. Somehow, without me even realizing it, God had quietly taken away my bitterness and anger, leaving a sense of calm in their place.

Though my wound is still visible, it didn't bother me the way it had before. It felt less like a reminder of pain and more like a testament to my strength.

I even found the courage to pray for my attacker, asking God to bring healing to her broken soul, who had caused me harm. And he did, something even more profound took place. The scar on my face became a bridge—a reminder of the journey from pain to forgiveness, a journey that allowed me to experience a part of God's grace.

Forgiveness transformed and gave me a deep sense of peace, an unshakable resilience, and even the ability to help others who wrestled with their own anger. My scar remained, but it was no longer a mark of shame or pain. Instead, it was a badge of my healing, a testimony of God's ability to turn wounds into wisdom and pain into peace.

Jackie Otto

https://www.linkedin.com/in/jackie-otto/
https://www.facebook.com/profile.php?id=61559998884421

My name is Jackie Otto, and I am entering my 30th year as a certified special education teacher. My training as a special educator helped me navigate my life at home with a husband who has a severe Traumatic Brain Injury (TBI).

We rescued a Black Mouth Cur/Mastiff blind dog, named Slider, and he is also my husband's comfort dog.

I am a lover of life, learning and making each day better for everyone that I encounter. I am certified now in a course where artistic expression blends with self-development. I'm excited for this new journey of helping others become the best version of themselves. Follow me soon on social media under Doodle and Discover Yourself with Jackie.

The Day That Changed Forever

By Jackie Otto

It was February 10, 2011, and it was the day that would forever change our lives as we knew it.

It was 10:00 AM and I was at work at the public school district where I have worked for the past 25 years. At the time, I was an LRS (Learning Resource Specialist) and had thirteen schools in my zone. I worked with those schools and helped teachers with classroom management, students' behavior, and anything else that was requested by teachers and/or administration within those schools.

I have had substantial experience with behavior over my 30 years in education. For my special education internship, I chose the most challenging class in Key Largo so I would get outstanding experience, and somehow, my life always seems to cycle back to behavior.

Anything having to do with behavior is, in fact, my love, and I would have no idea how much I would need all that training on such a personal level very soon.

I was at one of my schools and in a former colleague's office, catching up on her life for a moment before I started my day when my cell phone rang. It was the school where my office was located, and the gal said that a police officer had been trying to get ahold of me and there had been an accident. After I hung up, all I could think of was, "An accident? A car accident? What kind of accident?" I couldn't calm my racing heart.

My world stopped as my friend tried to console me and help me figure out the next steps. I decided to call the sheriff's office and try to track down the officer. As soon as I dialed, my phone rang again. This time, it was the police officer. He said my husband had been in an accident, and I needed to meet them at Lee Memorial Hospital in Ft Myers (which is a Level II trauma center) and that the EMTs and paramedics were trying to stabilize him. My recollection is that he concluded with the words, it doesn't look good when asked if he would be OK.

What he did not tell me is that my husband had fallen off our roof at home, and that his prognosis was not good. Slider passed away 12/21/24 and on 1/19/25 we rescued a Black Mouth Cur puppy, and her name is Hudini AKA: Dini. She is bringing fresh energy into our home.

My mind raced.

Is this the way they tell you your husband didn't make it until you arrive at the hospital in person?

My friend grabbed her belongings and, without another word, said, "Where are we going?" Lee Memorial Hospital was my answer. I did have some feeling of relief knowing that it is one of the best trauma centers in the state of Florida, and they have an amazing reputation and air flight patients from many out of area locations.

That car ride was a complete blur to me, and I'm not sure what the conversation was, if there even was any.

I do remember not being able to get there fast enough: red lights, stop signs, and people driving slowly, but at the same time, I was also terrified of taking my first step into that hospital – into the unknown.

Being left with my own thoughts during times of crisis is beyond terrifying.

Once we finally arrived, the doors opened into the ER, and I announced who I was to the lady behind the window. She told me to have a seat.

Have a seat?

Did she know what had happened to my husband?

Have a seat, I repeated in my head.

As my mind raced and raced as to what I would encounter once someone would talk to me was more than my mind could manage.

I now understood how people fainted when they received terrifying news. My head was buzzing with the present moment, the sights and smells of the ER, and especially the unknown.

I hardly made it to a chair when I heard my name being called. Another friend, who was an Assistant Principal at another school at the time, met us at the hospital. I remember they both stood one on each side as Kathy, the social worker, reeled off the long list of injuries that my husband had sustained during his fall off our roof.

Broken neck

Broken back

Broken clavicle

Fractured spine (several spots)

Fractured ribs

Fractured wrist

Collapsed lung

Possible Brain Injury (TBI) with a brain bleed

With a broken back and broken neck, I wondered if he was paralyzed. Thankfully, when I asked the doctor, he reassured me that he was not.

His brain bleed was the biggest concern of all. The rest would heal, but, what about his brain?

I went to see him and walked right past him several times, lying on a gurney. At that time, after twenty years together, I didn't even recognize my husband with his swollen face, swollen head, swollen body, and the many attached machines that were now part of my husband Mark.

Time stood still, and I am sure I did, too.

I dropped my head, looked closer, and it still did not look like him, and I didn't recognize anything about him except his clothes. I knew those were his clothes, so I guess it must be Mark.

Was that really him?

I was speechless and offered a few encouraging words that I cannot recall besides, I love you!

I am a talker and joke that I can talk to a rock. Well, I would need to be that rock, and I had no idea how profound that thought would become.

The trauma doctor said, "We've got to go to surgery - now!" I watched as they whizzed my husband's gurney right past me and out of the ER. It looked like he was being kept alive by machines.

I was frozen in time.

Was he alive, or were the machines breathing for him?

What was next?

Would he live?

Did he even know I was there?

What should I do now?

My mind was whirling around with too many what-ifs and with so many unimaginable emotions, and the pessimistic thoughts would not stop.

I asked my friends to repeat what the social worker had said, as I had not comprehended this information.

I was still traumatized by the thought of not recognizing my husband.

My world had come to a dead standstill for the moment, as well as the next three hours while he underwent emergency surgery for his brain bleed. I had a choice... I could pace the floor of the trauma waiting room and create grooves in the floor, or I could go get my car and try to stay busy.

I could not, and would not, stand and pace the floor for the next three hours. I would be next in surgery if I had to stay there, left to my own thoughts.

I had my friend drive me back to school in Lehigh, where I received the dreaded call so I could retrieve my car before they locked the school up for the night.

I called my sister-in-law. She is always calm and rational. I told her what had happened to her brother. She said she would pack and be on her way.

It is about a three-and-a-half-hour drive from Homestead to Fort Myers by car, so I had some time to waste.

I retrieved my phone charger, and as I was driving into our complex, Linda, a neighbor, called out and asked if I needed help. I asked if she would ride with me to the hospital as I wasn't sure if I was even able to drive. She jumped in, and off we went.

She may need to be my driver, but I felt more in control of the situation while behind the wheel. It was the only thing that I could control at the time was driving my own car.

The only thing I picked up at my home was my cell phone charger. It would later prove to be my lifeline.

We made it back to the hospital with still an hour and a half of time left until Mark's surgery was to conclude, and once that time passed, I got more worried with each passing minute.

Finally, the neurosurgeon, Dr John Dusseau, came out to speak to me. Once he started talking, I immediately loved this man for his knowledge, patience, bedside manner, and being one of the kindest doctors that I have encountered in the medical field.

He performed a craniotomy on Mark, where they took a bone flap out to allow room for his damaged/traumatized brain to swell, his TBI was considered a severe traumatic brain injury.

I would later find out that they didn't want to put the bone flap into his abdomen, which is fairly common, so they had to put it in the freezer for preservation.

That has remained a running joke with us to this day.

Once my sister-in-law Martha got there, I felt like she would help me stay calm and help me understand what the doctors were saying. It is so easy to misunderstand any and all information when your emotional state is heightened.

My friend Pat brought me a blank journal and told me to write everything down: what the doctors say, questions I have, thoughts, and things to look up.

This would be some of the best advice I received during this crisis.

We were told 72 hours would be the magic number to see how Mark's brain was healing. We were also told that his brain had shifted to one side of his brain stem. The three days dragged on as we anxiously waited to find out what would happen next.

They told us that he was headed in the right direction.

Mark's son Justin flew in from New Hampshire, but I have no idea what day that was, nor did I write it down. I think it was about day three.

So much remains a blur.

I was hopeful yet annoyed each time the doctors responded with, "We don't know," to my endless questions. I was happy that it wasn't a completely discouraging answer, yet I felt the need to want a tangible answer all at the same time.

We would get through one hurdle, only to have another hurdle rear its ugly head. I review my blank book. As I read today what I wrote thirteen years ago, I am reminded how very fortunate we all really are, and that all the hurdles we actually jumped through courageously.

Mark was in Lee Memorial Hospital for fifteen days. We then transferred him to Sarasota to a rehab hospital where he spent the next thirty days. He woke up from his coma on March 11, 2011, which happened to be Fat Tuesday. New Orleans is our favorite city, so I found this to be fitting.

Happy Fat Tuesday, Mark!

He then headed back to Lee Memorial for a cranioplasty to put the bone flap back in. There were many hurdles in the way of the next step, which was to get him to Atlanta to a specialty hospital.

I chartered a plane so that he could attend Shepherd Center in Atlanta. The Shepherd Center is a specialty hospital for spinal cord and brain injury. Mark ended up in the dual diagnostic ward because that was the only bed open at the time.

Mark eventually recovered and healed from many of his injuries except his severe brain injury. That is something that we still manage daily. Some days are fine, and many are challenging.

Hope and prayers are what keeps us going.

There were moments of setbacks and re-dos. I had to practice patience, patience, and more patience.

You get to know people and their stories while in these situations. You also come to know the families of those who did not make it.

Thank God, Mark had a better outcome than many.

The moments turned into days that turned into setbacks and high fives, joys, tears, and, at times, downright discouragement.

There are days that we are content and silly. And there are days that are filled with repetition, irritation, frustration, wonder, anxiety, panic, apprehension, worry, nervousness, trepidation, and unease.

Being a caregiver is one of the hardest jobs on the planet, BUT, no matter what, I have never chosen to give up. Till death do us part are very powerful words that are only reviewed amongst the most challenging of times.

I am strong for Miracle Man Mark every day, and there are days that I take it one moment at a time because one day at a time is way too overwhelming. At times, I don't know how I managed through the last thirteen years. I'd love to say I did it with grace, but there are days that it doesn't look or feel like grace.

But, one thing I know for sure is that if I can manage this, so can you!

As Winnie the Pooh so eloquently said, "You are braver than you believe, stronger than you seem, smarter than you think, and loved more than you know."

Heather D. Mahoney

Founder of Success Strategies Advisors, Inc.

https://www.linkedin.com/in/heatherdmahoney/
https://www.facebook.com/RoadmapHeather/
https://www.instagram.com/Roadmapheather/
https://roadmapheather.com/

Heather D. Mahoney is a Certified Life Coach and Certified Passion Test Facilitator who works with women stuck at a crossroads; together, they design a roadmap to the destination they've always dreamed of. Her journey began when she realized she had been living according to what she thought others expected of her rather than by being true to her authentic self. She changed direction and is now a successful business owner and published author. To help others who've reached a similar dead end, she wrote "Designing Your Life's Roadmap: 8 Pathways to Guide Your Exit from the Pretender Highway" (available on Amazon). Besides her life coaching business, she owns and operates a home healthcare agency for people with memory issues.

Heather is a U.S. Army veteran. She lives in Hollywood, Florida, with her dog, Henley, and her son, Emerson, when he's home from college.

When My American Dream Died, I Rose from the Ashes

By Heather D. Mahoney

The day I almost died in childbirth was the day my real life began. It was the day I finally began to come out of the waking coma that had engulfed me for years. The day I began to rise from the ruins of a life I was never meant to live.

In 2004, when I was seven months pregnant, my doctor discovered I had uncontrollable high blood pressure, which put me at risk for a life-threatening condition called eclampsia. He ordered me to go straight to the hospital, where my son, Emerson, was delivered by emergency Cesarean section – two months premature. I immediately fell into a coma and didn't know he had been born until I woke up a week later.

This shattering experience was literally a wake-up call. Facing death will make you confront some hard truths, and my truth was that I had been living inauthentically for years, pursuing material possessions to satisfy the world and what I thought it expected of me. I loved my son, but the career, husband and house I had worked so hard to get now meant nothing to me.

So what did I want?

I began asking myself that question, and for the first time in my life, I started answering it honestly.

Is this what I wanted?

No.

Living the Wrong Plan

I don't remember how I came to believe in the importance of having the "right" job and a home full of sleek material possessions. Growing up, I saw the dream promoted wherever I looked.

I saw smiling, happy people having the time of their lives. There they were, splashed across the glossy pages of the magazines or shimmering in the glow of the TV screen. They wore the most fabulous clothes, drove the coolest cars and drank the most delicious cocktails or soda. They spent their days and nights having so much more fun than I did – why couldn't I live like that?

No one in my life told me it was all just an entertaining fantasy and that I should pursue a more meaningful life. Certainly not my mother, who never really said anything about anything except to make the most basic comments about the food, shelter and clothing she provided. We had about five topics we could talk about with her, and the weather was probably the most interesting of them.

The gifts we gave her never seemed to please her. She didn't criticize them; she just accepted them passively, not showing emotion. Perhaps that explains my materialism. Was my acquisitiveness a hopeless quest to prove I deserved her love?

I left home as soon as I was old enough to enlist in the U.S. Army, used my military benefits to get bachelor's and master's degrees in management fields, and married as soon as I found someone with whom I believed I could live my dream of an ideal relationship: a best friend to grow old with.

The marriage was good enough for me, at least. We fit each other and got along, I suppose, because we had the same superficial standards. He wanted a wife who made good money and took care of a big house that showed how successful we were.

It was all good enough until Emerson was born, and the façade began to fall.

Good Enough Is Not Enough

After I woke up from the coma, I went home, but Emerson remained in the hospital for three more weeks. It took me a year to fully recover. I was moody and depressed, unable to focus on anything but how to get through the next few hours. I wasn't eating and couldn't sleep, even with the pills my doctor prescribed, because I was sure I would die if I went to sleep.

At the same time, I was handling most of the care of Emerson and the household. I would work all day and come home to more work – what women often call "the second shift." Rightly or wrongly, I blamed him for the fact that all the work seemed to be falling on me. I know he was struggling and stressed out, too, and I wasn't blameless. But we had such poor communication skills that we couldn't talk it out and get to a better place.

My unhappiness was starting to push through the veneer of contentment I had erected. Then, I lost my job as a human resources executive. I should have been upset, after all the work I had put in to get it and keep it. But, like my marriage, it was just a status symbol I was hiding behind to make the world think I was a success. I was a college graduate; I was supposed to dress up every day, go to an office, and make Important Decisions. I played the part, but all it did was raise my blood pressure. It felt good to finally be liberated from the job that made me want to jump out of the window and die every single day.

Everything was a fight. I guess he saw me as too controlling, and maybe I was. But there seemed to be so little I could control!

As Emerson got older, things got worse. While I was up at four-thirty or five o'clock in the morning to get Emerson ready for school and make breakfast, the husband was sleeping. If I wanted something done around the house, he was busy. He would cut a friend's lawn while ours was growing over my head.

Before we became parents, it was OK if he didn't do something around the house. But now I needed him, and he wasn't there.

When I finally started coming out of my zombie state, I began to look at my life and examine what I wanted and didn't want. I knew I didn't want the life I was living, but I didn't know how to go forward and move away from it. It wasn't just easier and safer to stay with what I knew; I was ashamed about who I had become. Leaving would be an admission that I had failed. What would everyone say when they discovered I was a failure?

I tried to get a new job but never did go back to the high-powered executive life. I went on interviews but the hiring managers knew something I didn't: I simply didn't want their jobs.

I paid my share of our expenses with my savings and part-time jobs. The husband kept pushing me to find "real" work and was losing patience, but I couldn't rouse myself from my waking sleep.

Finally, the truth was impossible to ignore any longer.

The Façade Falls

First, my mother passed away. She had been in an assisted-living facility for memory care issues, and one day in 2013, she began suffering organ failure and was admitted to the hospital.

My sister and I rushed to her bed and watched her, a once-powerful woman who had towered over us our entire lives and now just lay there – not moving, not fighting, unable to do anything.

She took her last breath and was gone.

Honestly, I don't know any of the details about how her health deteriorated so quickly and fatally. That's how broken our relationship was. But I knew I didn't want my family to watch me die with the same lack of emotional connection.

I started thinking about the life I was not living and the one I wanted to live – truly live. I realized how much I wanted to do the things I dreamed of. I wanted to be true to myself.

Then, on a Wednesday night in 2014, my husband told me he had filed for divorce, and I would be served the following week. He was no longer willing to put up with my inability to work and the other lingering effects of the depression I suffered after nearly losing my life giving birth to our son.

I wasn't surprised, and strangely, I wasn't heartbroken over losing this man I never should have married in the first place. My strongest emotions were shame and embarrassment at failing in everything society said were the only things that mattered. I was a little relieved that I was finally being taken out of the situation I was so unhappy in.

There was no pretending anymore. I had no job. My mother had died. I had a son in an expensive private school I couldn't afford and a mortgage I could barely pay. My husband was leaving me and taking away my only steady source of financial support. (He thought public school was good enough and that the mortgage providing his son's home was somehow not his responsibility.)

What was I going to do?

Creating My Plan

The first thing I did was to figure out what I wanted, a new exercise, considering I had lived my whole life figuring out how to help others get what they wanted. I wanted three things:

First, I wanted to keep Emerson in his school, where he was getting an excellent education. He had found a second family there, a warm, nurturing environment he would need to help him cope with the breakup of his family.

Second, I wanted to keep the house. I couldn't take away the only home Emerson had ever known, and I liked building equity in my own property instead of throwing away my money on rent every month. Emerson didn't deserve to lose his home because of his parents' failure.

Third, I wanted a flexible schedule that would allow me to spend time with Emerson. I needed to pay the bills, but not at the expense of my relationship with him. I didn't want a 9-to-5 job because I wanted to be involved in my son's elementary and middle school years.

I decided the only way I could meet all three goals was to work for myself. I started a residential cleaning service and a resume writing/interview company. It wasn't easy to juggle the two businesses and be responsible for all the legal and financial requirements of owning a company, but I had the flexibility I needed for Emerson. This was my No. 1 priority.

Keeping the mortgage and the private school was the right thing for Emerson, even though it went against my financial interest. So, I forged ahead. I didn't always pay the bills on time, but I got them paid one way or another. I worked out a plan with Emerson's school; the administrators kindly worked with me so they could keep him as a student. I finished paying them the December after he graduated from eighth grade.

And all that worrying about what other people would think? I look back on it now and I realize few people gave it any thought. People expressed sorrow at the breakup, wished me well and went on with their lives.

One friend did notice. "You don't look angry anymore," she said.

Finding a New Path

For the first time, I had the control I needed over my own life – mostly. I couldn't control everything.

For the first three years, I felt like I was always behind. That was very difficult because, until that point, I had never had a problem with credit. If I saw something I wanted, I went ahead and purchased it without any challenge. Now, when financial emergencies surprised me, I had to take on more debt or borrow money from family members as a last resort. But I was making progress.

I am emotionally, financially and professionally secure. I have so many options. The best part is just that I get to enjoy this extraordinary life. It's not always easy. But I'm happy to be where I am, with all the lessons learned. I really came into my own once I let go of the perception that what other people believe matters.

What helped me a great deal was The Passion Test, a tool that helps someone make decisions, create a plan and eliminate false beliefs, ideas and concepts. One of its premises is to focus on where you want to go without worrying about the individual steps you take to get there. Everything will unfold as it needs to. I was so very stuck in that process kind of thinking: *What is step one? Step 2? Step 3? I did Step 3 before Step 2 – is that OK? Am I doing any of this right?*

Now, I just look where I want to end up and understand that everything else will fall into place.

I've learned to think with my heart instead of my head. Using my head is how I got into a dissatisfied life, a bad marriage and an unfulfilling career.

I want you to find the same fulfillment.

Dig deep within yourself to find what you want – not what you think you should want, but what you truly want. Be open to what the universe brings you and use it to tap into your desires.

Understand that you can't achieve anything by yourself. You need a partner, male or female, who can help you find your way – a navigator who provides accountability and shares your wind with you.

The Journey Continues

In the process of pursuing my authentic dreams, I found my voice and started to live. I came to realize I had passions, too, and it was OK to pursue them. When I pursued them, I was happy. At the same time, I was fulfilling my mission of self-fulfillment, my obligation to myself.

I'm so grateful that I was forced to reroute from my dead end and find a new way forward. It's a route open to anyone willing to ask themselves what they want and then go after it.

Eight years after the night I was informed of the divorce and worried that I'd have to put Emerson in public school, I watched him graduate from his private school. Soon after, he started college with his entire education paid for, debt-free, with a fund I had been carefully nurturing since he was born.

Two years after that, I paid off the mortgage on my house and have started focusing on future wealth.

I own two successful businesses, including one that helps other women design their life's roadmap when they're feeling overwhelmed and struggling with making decisions, the lack of a plan, feelings of isolation and the belief that "I can't." I guide my clients with what I learned while redesigning my life's roadmap; those lessons became the basis of an interactive workbook I published in 2022.

I appreciate every hiccup and every poor decision that brought me here. I'm grateful to be where I am – living life on my terms and feeling joy about who I am and where I am.

My life had crumbled into ashes, but it took a near-death experience and the final demise of my marriage before I saw it. Then, I rose from the ashes like a phoenix and created something new and far more wonderful.

If you can create a more fulfilling life and give yourself permission to go after it, there's nothing you can't achieve.

Stephanie Owens

Owner and CEO of LoLo's Sweet-Cakes & Catering LLC

http://www.linkedin.com/in/dr-stephanie-owens-1a568037
https://www.facebook.com/stephanie.owens.39142
https://lolossweetcakesandcatering.com/

Dr. Stephanie Owens is known as a transformational leader, entrepreneur, and former teen-age mother. Born in Crescent City, Florida, she dreamed of becoming an author. She began writing as an adolescent due to low self-esteem. She believed her dark skin, nappy hair, and buck teeth made her unworthy of the attention of others. Through years of perseverance, Dr. Owens was able to overcome obstacles. The daughter of teenage parents, she was determined to end the generational cycle.

A professionally trained educator, Dr. Owens, has spent the last 30 years thriving in education (K-12). Educated at two major universities, she earned a Bachelors, Masters, Educational Specialist, and Doctorate Degree. She spent those years working as a cafeteria worker, teacher, coach, and administrator. She has earned prestigious honors: Secondary ESE Administrator of the Year, National Life Group Life Changer of the Year, Coach of the Year, and Whose Who Among American Teachers.

Teen Mom

By Stephanie Owens

"She won't do anything with her life", a Christian woman in the community said. She won't do anything, but be on welfare and have a lot of babies for different men!

"She's so fast, you are not allowed to be around her" a mother of one of my friends said.

What was I thinking? When I look back, I was not thinking at all. This couldn't be happening. This had to be a cruel joke. Growing up in a small town in rural Florida, everyone knew everyone. Raised in the Pentecostal Church there was strict doctrine. We were taught to have great values and morals. How did I find myself in such mess? I had made the biggest mistake of my young life. I was pregnant! A million thoughts were in my head. What was I going to do? "My family will be disappointed". How am I going to explain? It all proved too much for my young mind to process. It was easier for me to act like things were normal. I continues to live my life as usual. Running, jumping, and playing hard. I hid my secret by eating very little and not sharing my sin. My mother always told me that I couldn't do what other kids did because I was different. She was very hard on me as I was not allowed to have a boyfriend or go to many peoples homes. In a rebellious state I ran away. I said, I can do what I want.... doing what I wanted meant being persuaded to do something I never had. The guy was not my boyfriend, I didn't even like him. It was the trick of the enemy. How stupid could be? I was not sexually active in other words I was a virgin.

During that time, I represented teenagers who faced being pregnant at a young age. Teen mothers are not the same but are unique in their own right.

Being in the 11th grade and pregnant was my reality. Pregnancy comes with stigma and backlash. I was already a daughter of unmarried of parents. My dad was 18 and my mom was 15 when I was born. The shame was unbearable, but God sustained me. The pain was both physical and mental. I already had no self esteem. What will everyone think about me after they find out? I cried, Lord help me! I don't want a baby. I don't love this man and he doesn't love me. The experience itself was traumatic. The pain was excruciating. No foreplay. No kissing. No penetration. How? Had I ruined my life?

Hiding my pregnancy became more difficult . My flat stomach started to become round. I wore a big jacket in efforts of concealing my big secret. My friends suspected but my mother had no clue.

27 weeks into my pregnancy, I experienced a medical emergency. I had an abruption. My placenta left early and I was bleeding to death... concerned about my mother and how she would feel. I asked that she not be notified. My secret, was no longer a secret. Everyone was finally going to know what I had been hiding and ignoring. The laundromat attendant replied again, "would you like me to call someone". I repeated, no! I had a calmness about me. Though blood poured down my legs. I kept my composure. I tried hard not to bring attention to myself. I was initially standing but I pulled myself up onto the table in efforts of minimizing the lost of blood. I said could you please call the ambulance. The ambulance was called and arrived a short time later. I was stabilized. What's going on? I said, I'm pregnant. How far along are you? 27 weeks, I mumbled. By that time we were off to the hospital.

The ride felt like a year but was only 30 drive by ambulance. When I arrived, I was prepped for emergency surgery. My life was in jeopardy as well the life of my unborn child. In my mind I still couldn't process I was having a baby. I couldn't process what was going on. I was very calm. My composure was puzzling for the EMT's. They thought that I

She Defies | 129

was in shock. I was not in shock, I had no feelings. I didn't know what to feel. I didn't know if I was going to live. I didn't know if the baby would live. I didn't know if I wanted to live. Later, I was told that I didn't bleed to death because I remained calm. By the grace of God we both made it. My baby girl and I were okay. She weighed 3 lbs but was healthy. So small she fit into a small shoe box. My heart was full. I went from being a teenager to being a teen mom. My mission in life changed instantly. This is something bigger than me. Someone is going to be depending on me. I started to think about what I would do with my life. How could I be a provider for my baby.

Shortly after my mother and grandmother arrived at the hospital. My grandmother never showed her disappointment in me. I held my head down in shame. If having a baby as a teenager and being unmarried is the worst thing you've done you're still good, my grandmother said. Hold your head up! My mama cried, not because I had a baby but because I had to go through the whole thing alone. She was hurt because I didn't trust her enough to let her know. Even though having a baby is not ideal at this point you don't have to worry about anything. This is me and your baby, said my mother. Both my grandmother and mother showed an unwavering love and support for me. Somehow the shame, fear, sadness, anger, disappointment in myself didn't seem so overwhelming within my family dynamics. We managed to move forward in love as a family. My family was actually amazing. My mother allowed to be a kid and assumed the roll of mothering my daughter. In spite of their support I continued to feel less than my peers. I felt judged and that nobody believed in me. The weight sometimes felt unbearable. I felt like an epic failure. Failure in my walk with Christ was the most challenging part of my sin. My other sins didn't leave reminders. I could repent and then go on with my life. Having a baby however meant that my community would remember me as the fast girl who had a baby in high school. Even as a child I had a great relationship with God. I wanted to please Him. My spirit grieved when I became pregnant. I knew He was so disappointed. I was disappointed! I couldn't forgive myself. So why would He? It was feeling I couldn't shake. I always felt like an outcast and like people were only tolerating me. I never fit in. Not fully understanding how I put myself and family in a position of disgrace. I pretended to be ok but I really wasn't. I perceived my self as the ugly duckling. Undesirable, Unloveable, unworthy are a few emotions that were always present. I was all ways embarrassed to tell someone I had a daughter from fear of being judged. I did offer the information but If asked, how old are you kids I would reluctantly say their ages. I wasn't ashamed of her, I was ashamed of myself.

When I think about it. Having a baby only added on to my insecurities. I had never felt good about myself. My skinny legs, my buck teeth, and my dark skin always made me feel insecure. In reflection, I can honestly say that the mistake I made stemmed from a need to be accepted. Since I can remember, all I wanted was somebody to want me, love me. I asked , Lord, why was I put on this earth? Was it to

experience such pain and loneliness. When children are products of teenage parents themselves there are other emotions and situations that the child encounters because their parents were children themselves. Absolutely in my situation I was exposed to so much. My grandparents were at odds. My paternal grandmother denied me from the beginning. She said I was not my father's child. My maternal grandmother was livid because my mother was only 15 years old. I can remember when I was about 9 or 10, wanting to visit her. She was always stone faced and never welcoming. She laughed and talked with my brothers but ignored me. My father 18 at the time my mother got pregnant moved away and I rarely saw him. I never talked to him unless he came to our town to visit my grandmother. It would be on Christmas. I can't remember ever getting any presents but I remember him coming to take me over to his mother's house. I met his three oldest sons there, my brothers . My grandmother was smitten with them. I could feel she didn't want me there but each time he came to visit I wanted to go. My mother by that

She Defies | 131

time was in a relationship with my brother's father. She was young and doing her own thing so I was left with my maternal grandmother while she traveled from state to state with my brothers and their dad working in different crops. Their father was a migrant contractor and they did this for most of my elementary school years. On a couple occasions she took me with her but it was never for long. I would end up back with my grandmother. She not only left me with my grandmother she left me other places with people who she thought she could trust. I endured a tremendous amount of pain and struggle to like myself. I was molested by three men as young girl. This was ongoing and scary! I hated to go to bed at night and was afraid to move because I was in fear of waking my abusers. I was a bed wetter but only when I was in places with my abusers. I eternalized my feelings for so long. As a child I was confused and as an adults the things that I endured continued to affect me. My experiences cemented the mistrust of men, feelings of unworthiness, feelings of not being wanted, and self persecution in my head. Intimacy was and has remained a struggle. Rejection has been an issue since my inception and I wrestle with it. The need of being wanted persists. I always felt like I was on the outside looking in. The first child of my mother and father. They both had offered children after me. Leaving me and doing life with their new family.

I am a testament to the lifelong struggles one faces when the parents are teenagers and unmarried. I couldn't find my place in the world and wanting to be wanted compromised my judgment . Additionally, an absent biological father made me yearn for attention. Though my stepfather was in the home and treated me well. I felt like a third wheel. I always wondered why I was never put first. When I took time to examine my heart. I realized the need to forgive myself. Mistakes are made. Those mistakes can either break you are make you. I began to believe that I can walk through life or l could let life walk over me. I'm reminded and I often quote to my students that we are free to make choices but we are never free of the consequences of those choices.

My Reason

My daughter made her entrance into the world. I had to get myself together. Because people in my community counted me out. I was only out if I wanted to be out! I began to remember my upbringing, my roots, my foundation, which is in God. I knew that God is the author and finisher of my faith. He's my alpha and omega. My beginning and my end. It's also, when I learned to trust God for myself. No longer operating on my mother and grandmother's faith I need to know him for myself. I resorted to my faith to be able to move forward. I said I am strong and through a Christ I can do anything. I've endured so much but can't continue to be pitiful. I have someone depending on me.

My daughter did not ask to enter the world. When she arrived, I took a new lease on life. Looking at her I knew I wanted to become more. How would I accomplish more? I had no idea. At the end of my 11th grade year I was still struggling with who I was. My mom continued to reassure me but being a mother was surreal. My mother was a champion for me and for my daughter. I was grateful that she allowed me to be a kid and experienced all the things kids my age were experiencing at the time. I still had a hard time accepting scrutiny from those in my community. It angered me but fueled me at the same time. I overheard on several occasions what others felt about me having a baby. Those comments, along with many others added to my pain and feelings of not being good enough. I wondered why my life took this path. Was God punishing me? I remember, I did not want to live. What was the big deal. Teenage girls have babies every day. The big deal was that I was considered a church girl. Pure in every aspect. I had fallen out of my communities good grace. A simple life became so much more complicated. I had to figure out how to move forward. I picked myself up and decided what I wanted to do with my life. I had so much more to work for... I attended summer school in order to be able to graduate on with my senior class. 12th grade came and went. I played volleyball, basketball, and softball and I was nominated to participate on the home coming court. Then I was selected Ms. Congeniality by the homecoming court. I enjoyed prom, homecoming, and grad night . 12th grade was absolutely amazing! It was one of the best times in my life. Things began to fall in line. My mind was made up and I was determined to not be a statistic. I applied to College! Because sadly, not one person asked me if I wanted to go to college. I did not let that deter me. When I left for college, my daughter was 18 months old. As a freshman I was mandated to stay on campus. I scheduled all of my classes Monday through Thursday and returned home at the end of the day on Thursdays. I returned to campus on Monday morning. Additionally, I had try outs for the volleyball team. I was selected to be on the teams. Not only was a student I was a college athlete. I didn't let what I had going on deter me from being a present mother. During volleyball season I traveled with the team. All classes were scheduled to ensure that I bonded with my daughter. It was important for me to lay a foundation for a better life . I attended college majoring in business administration and marketing. I was focused on bettering our situation, by educating myself. I wanted to be present and intentional. Every decision I made from that point, was made with my daughter in mind. She was perfect. Her hair was dark and silky. Her little fingers were perfect. My heart screamed with love for this little bundle of joy. My mistake started to feel less like a mistake. I called her my reason. My drive and my determination. My reason to always do better. My reason for not giving up. She had become my motivation. I wanted to make her proud and I wanted to prove to my community that life is not determined by the mistakes that one makes. I felt obligated to my baby and to myself to make their conversations a lie. Had I not gotten pregnant at a young age I know I wouldn't have the drive and determination that I have. Adversity, trials, tribulations and obstacles helped me see a clearer path. When I felt like giving up. I reflected on the strength it took for me to go through a teenage pregnancy alone. It's funny how life has a way of changing us for the better. Things I thought

I would die from only made me stronger. Life's situations can be a test. The strength I exhibited as a young girl was the strength I've needed through out my life. It was never easy to share my heart with others. It had been broken time and time again. In all my struggles Hod has sustained me. When k was at my lowest he was there to pick me up. He's never failed nor forsaken me. God believed in me when I didn't believe in myself. He loved me when I didn't love myself. He wiped my tears away in the most trying times in my life. He was and has been my foundation. The grace He gave me is the grace I give others. When I started trust

"She believed she could so she did".

My Life Speaks for Itself

A professional in the public school system I have a great career. Working in many capacities. Teacher, coach, and administrator. Empowered,

I graduated with my Bachelor's Degree, Master's Degree, Educational Specialist Degree, and Doctorate Degree. A life long learner I have strived to be a light. I have used my pass as experiences to catapult be ahead in life. The never give up spirit that I acquired as a teenager abides with me today. If God did it then will do it now. He's the same God yesterday, today, and forever. A licensed insurance agent and aspiring investment broker the pain I experienced has been replaced by love and security. A small business owner and entrepreneur I set my sights on financial security into my retirement. I find so much joy in helping families with financial literacy. My professional back ground and education has allowed me to serve in numerous capacities. Constantly engaged in seeking and taking advantage of opportunities to expand my knowledge and skills has proved to beneficial. Motivated, I have worked extremely hard to accomplish the goals which I have set . Although I faced many challenges along the way, I never succumbed to having a "quitting spirit". My positive attitude and willingness to do whatever it takes to achieve my goals has guided me over the years.

My Extensive knowledge as it relates to Exceptional Student Education I have been a great resource for teachers, parents, and children alike. As a mentor, volunteer, and coach I have dedicates my time and talent. My acknowledgment of my beloved Zeta Phi Beta Sorority Inc. instills 4 principles that I live by: Sisterhood, Service , Scholarship and Finer Womanhood . Committed, dedicated, self-motivated, trustworthy, and a self starter, all qualities I possess are based on my unwavering desire to defy the odds places on me by others.

So much for small beginnings and other people determining what you can do and who you can be.

Suzanne E. Minshew

Founder of Zannie Goods

https://www.facebook.com/suzanne.minshew
https://www.instagram.com/zannie_minshew/

Suzanne is a wife, mom of 3 and grandma to 2, and loves the Lord and her family beyond measure. She has a BA from Hiram College and has had a successful career in management, recruiting and career coaching as well as Healthcare with smatterings of volunteer work focused primarily on fundraising. Throughout her career she has been afforded the opportunity to do extensive amounts of writing from standard orders of procedures and company policies to employee hero stories and media releases. She has rekindled a love of writing and is developing a portfolio of poetry and short stories, which she will hopefully share with the world one day. Her biggest passion is healing and helping those along their own journey of healing. After a tumultuous upbringing and many mistakes along the way, she has focused her adult life on trusting the Lord and finding healing for herself, mentally, physically, emotionally and spiritually. Her prayer is that you find some nugget of healing or inspiration within her writings to find healing for yourself.

Overcoming and Healing

By Suzanne E. Minshew

Are you searching for answers? Seeking something to help ease the terrible pain that you are in? Are you attempting to make the chaos of your life stop or at least slow down so that you can catch your breath? Whatever the reason, I welcome you and pray that you will find some nugget of truth in my story to help you along your way to freedom, healing and blessing. Here is my story and some principles that I have adopted along the way for healing and creating a new life for myself.

There have been many starts and restarts in my life as I have grown, learned and matured, but there is one particular time in my life that I consider truly pivotal. If I had continued on the path that I was on in my early mid-20s, I would not be here today. Fear, shame and bad decisions were a way of life for me. As a child of a single mother alcoholic, my early years were filled with instability, living with different family members, filled with uncertainty and while there were no made-for-TV scenes that played out, the behaviors and attitudes that were created in me early on set me on a path of self-destruction later. I was a victim, an innocent child, filled with longing. Longing to be loved, to be encouraged, to be valued, accepted, something, anything. I was alone much of the time: left to my own mind and my own devices. When I reached adolescence, this longing turned into feeling unworthy of love or anything good, self-loathing and general disrespect for myself and for others. I was desperate to be loved. I suppose I knew that God loved me, but who could truly love me if I hated myself? I lived and made decisions according to these beliefs. There were some good, but mostly desperate attempts to be liked or loved.

When I went off to college, it was a fresh start, except that I took myself and my longing and self-hatred with me. I worked hard and performed like I was expected to on the surface. I smiled and made friends, tried new things, got good grades and was involved in as much as I could to keep myself busy. Too busy, as by spring, I had completely worked myself into a state of exhaustion and had lost relationships, because how could I possibly have any healthy, lasting relationships when I wasn't worthy of them anyway? The pattern continued, but with the help of one of my professors, I was able to do some self-work to lessen my theatrics and settle into college life. There were still ups and downs, some bridges burned; I struggled with depression, and 6 credits from graduating, I just simply gave up and wandered. I worked in Canada for about a year, chasing love. Came back to the US after a drunken ATV accident and was back in my mother's home, which was not good for me. Once healed enough to work, I began working at a hotel about 45 minutes from home. I found a room to rent and tried going back to school to finish my final credits for graduation. Enter an ex-boyfriend from high school (not my school) who seemed to enjoy my brokenness and to see me struggle. He said all the right things, and even though he cheated on me in high school, I fell for his words of manipulation and allowed him into my life. This was the final chapter before hitting rock bottom. The next two years were filled with complete and utter chaos. After moving in with me, I soon discovered that, surprise, he's an alcoholic. He did get a job and quickly whisked me away to our own apartment, away from my supportive roommates. My schooling fell by the wayside when he was fired. There were beatings and bruises, broken bones and trips to the ER. I was housed by Catholic Charities to keep me safe, only to go back to him over and over. He permitted me to go to work, but I couldn't see my friends. I was threatened and ridiculed and told I was worthless. All these things were confirmations of what I already believed about myself. And then, the pregnancy test was positive. I was terrified, but life became more manageable for a time. My partner found his way back to AA and experienced sobriety. I worked as much as I could while he focused on his program. Then, it was decided for me that we move closer to our families so that we could get help with the baby when the time came. So, we moved to a tiny little 2-bedroom duplex 20 minutes from my hometown. My commute to work was about 40 minutes, but it worked. The baby was induced on December 30th, and a drunken partner arrived at the hospital minutes before the birth. The arrival of my son was smooth, and I fell in love with him the moment they laid him in my arms. We returned to our tiny home with the baby, and I prayed. My mother had visited the hospital, and we began making efforts in our relationship. She called often to see how we were, and we visited a few times. My partner informed me that I would not be returning to work as my place was at home, and my car had been destroyed, so I quit my job. Three months went by, and my partner's drinking accelerated. I lived in fear and ensured I kept myself between him and my sweet boy. One day, in a tirade, my partner threw me against the wall with the baby in my arms. It was as if a light switched on. What was I doing? I quickly came to my senses, and while the abuser was gone, I packed our things and called my mom. Surprisingly, she came to the rescue.

This was the beginning of my new life. It wasn't easy being back in my mother's home, with her judgment and drinking, coupled with threats and surprise visits from the ex-partner, but I learned quickly how to rise up and advocate for myself. In time, my mother's heart softened, and she became surprisingly supportive, though she made clear that she wanted no details of the horrors I had experienced. I attended Al-Anon, AA, or whatever 12-step program I could go to to begin healing. I was desperate to get off the carousel of self-destruction and be normal. I found a sponsor and began intensive therapy, going twice a week for over a year. My therapist, Janet Faye, was an incredible gift to me with her gentle demeanor and hippie vibe. She led me through the darkest part of my life, and for that, I am truly grateful. The people in the groups I was a part of became like family and were instrumental in my healing. They truly carried me, spoke truth into my life, directed me back to God and helped me begin to develop healthier ways of thinking about myself, others and the world. I did a lot of looking over my shoulder, but eventually, my abuser disappeared from town and my life, and I was able to breathe easier. I was almost free. I returned to school, got a part-time job and began making plans for the future, for me and for the boy who changed my life, who saved me.

As with life, my story continues for many more years, but this particular time in my life was truly a turning point to be able to attain the incredible life that I get to live today. Looking back, I see how sick I was and how it took all of those events to bring me to my knees, to surrender to God and put a fire in my belly for healing and moving forward. And how I was able to survive, find healing and be where I am today, is a miracle. If you are in an abusive situation, whether it be physically, mentally, or emotionally, please get yourself out. Call 911, ask for help from a friend, family member or neighbor. You do not deserve to be abused. You are beautiful and can have the life you have always dreamt of.

The healing process is sometimes difficult and a lifelong one, but worth every minute. For me, following some basic principles has been key for healing. First, trust God. He is the Creator of all things heaven and earth. He is the one who loves us so much that He sent His only son to earth to die for us. He is THE great healer and provider, and I have seen His work throughout my life. He protected me and kept me safe, guided me and put angels in my path to help me. Today He is my best friend and the one I go to first in everything. He is there for you, too, if you'll let Him.

Next, find healthy support for yourself. If you are blessed with family and friends who understand and can walk alongside you as you find healing, consider yourself blessed. One-on-one therapy was instrumental for me. My therapist helped me with codependency, setting boundaries, learning to value and care for myself first before sharing myself with another person, and so much more. If you have experienced trauma, I encourage you to find a therapist who specializes in EMDR (Eye Movement Desensitization and Reprocessing). This was not available to me when going through the healing from my upbringing and abuse, but it was very helpful when I experienced trauma later in life. Therapy for me has not been a "one and done" experience. Our lives are layered, kind of like an onion, so when you peel off one layer, there may be something lingering below that needs to be worked through. I have been in and out of therapy all of my adult life for different issues and have been freed from so much.

Beyond one-on-one therapy, attending groups that focus on whatever your issues (codependency, addiction, loss of a loved one, suicide survivor, etc.) can be helpful. For me, Al-Anon, AA and Celebrate Recovery have been instrumental in my healing. The rooms are filled with others who are either where you are or where you've been. It is very important to find a seasoned sponsor to walk the road with you and then, study and pray and learn your way to healing. Bible study groups have been a lifeline for me as well. While they are not focused on my issues, they are focused on God, and the more I learn about Him and His will for us, the more I heal. The Bible is filled with life stories of people overcoming obstacles and getting closer to God. The women in my current Bible study are the most loving, welcoming and encouraging women I have ever experienced. They fill gaps and make me desire to be a better human and a better follower of Christ.

The third principle is learning to like and ultimately love yourself. Take time to really learn about yourself. What do you like? What don't you like? While I was growing up, I never really knew what I liked because it was either dictated to me or I just wanted to be liked so much that I would change myself to fit the other person. It wasn't until I was going through therapy that I allowed myself to have a differing opinion, to explore what I liked and what I didn't and developed the ability to share it without feeling like I was going to be condemned or shamed for it. What a freeing experience it is! I have done this over and over throughout the years as with a husband and 3 growing sons, I was prone to losing myself in schedules, work and making sure that everyone else was taken care of. That refocus is life-giving.

Beyond liking yourself, how do you learn to love yourself? This can be tough. Explore what makes you happy, what brings you peace, contentment and fulfillment. For me, I write. I can take all the ugly feelings and negative thoughts as well as the overwhelming feelings of love and joy and get them out and on paper. It doesn't have to be pretty, it just has to be released. When I couldn't write, I did a visual journal, cutting out pictures and words from magazines to work out whatever I was going through. Gardening has become a beautiful part of my healing journey. I am a novice, but there is something so fulfilling in digging my hands in the dirt, planting something that will provide food or something beautiful, that gives me such joy and happiness. This year was a banner year for me. Lots of green beans, tomatoes and happy flowers. I also enjoy reading my Bible and praying. This is my most perfect lifeline to God, His will and how He feels about me.

In expanding my interests, I have learned to truly love myself through the success and failure processes. Failure used to be such a shameful thing for me. If I made a mistake or failed at something, it meant, in my head, that I was a total failure. Depression would set in, and self-defeating behaviors would emerge. Today, I can see that successes are wonderful, and I love them, and through failure, I experience the opportunity for growth. I learn something, and I move forward without beating myself up. Am I perfect at this? No, but I am so much better than I used to be. Do I like myself? Yes, most of the time. I'm human, I make mistakes, and then I move on. Do I love myself? Absolutely! I love that I have learned and grown and overcome so many obstacles. I love that I can love without desperately needing to be loved in return. I love that I actually like spending time with myself. I love that I am committed to the healing process and hold tight to the fact that I will be perfectly healed when I get to heaven.

The fourth principle is to keep moving forward. In the beginning, for me, it was like I had cement bricks on my feet, and it felt like I could not move forward, but by inches. What I know now is that if it were easy, I would have cast aside the process years ago and gone my own way, likely back into another unhealthy relationship. I shed a lot of tears in the beginning, by the bucket full, but I am thankful for every tear I shed, for each tear represented some tiny bit of healing that was occurring. A tiny release of pain. So, don't be discouraged, Trust God and keep moving forward, and in a year, 2 years, 5, 10, 20 years, you will be surprised at the progress you have made.

The principle I like most is to Celebrate. For a time, I needed to celebrate every tiny little movement that I made towards being a healthier person. Each time I was able to advocate for myself and say no without shame or guilt. Each time that I was able to look in the mirror and appreciate my own beauty looking back. Yes, even today, with the wrinkles and gray hair that I continue to battle. I celebrate that I can answer the phone without fear of who is on the other end of the line or that I can walk into the store and not see a face that feels unsafe to me. I celebrate the achievements I have made in writing, hiking, singing, and learning new things. I celebrate overcoming whatever obstacle presents itself. These are my celebrations. Yours are likely different, so celebrate, my friend, the beautiful, talented, God-given gift to the world that you are. Celebrate the release of fear, anxiety, shame, guilt, all of it! Whatever you have overcome, big or small, Celebrate! And if you can't do that yet, celebrate that in these 5 minutes, you haven't broken down in tears or succumbed to an addiction or allowed someone to hurt you. Baby steps and deep breaths to a celebration of you!

I pray that you have found something in my words that will help you along your healing journey. My story, to me, is a miracle, and I am so grateful that I was able to be freed from the burdens of self-destruction, self-loathing, etc. These principles do not have to be yours in totality.

You can adjust them to fit you and your situation or even develop your own. You are beautiful inside and out and are deserving of healing. You are loved deeply and completely, even if you don't realize it yet. Thank you for taking the time to walk with me through my story of overcoming and healing. Be blessed!

PS: To fill in some gaps in the story for you, the ex-partner was not in my eldest son's life. He chose drugs and alcohol and ultimately passed away from alcoholism. I graduated from college and took a job in Southern California, where I met my husband, who adopted my precious boy. That boy has grown into a remarkable man, with a lovely wife and 2 beautiful sons. We are so proud!

The relationship with my mother ebbed and flowed. I can only guess that with age and health issues, she gave up alcohol. With God and therapy, I was able to forgive her and develop a relationship. She lived with us for several years due to poor health and ultimately passed away. The final years with her gleaned some beautiful memories for my family. My relationship with her wasn't the way I would have liked as she was very closed off and protective of herself, but my security in my relationship with God and who I am allowed me to let go of any expectations and find comfort in knowing that I was doing what God called me to do in caring for her.

Ariel Balfour

Founder and CEO of Trauma 2 Triumph Coaching Inc.

https://www.facebook.com/ariel.sommers/
https://www.instagram.com/thearielbalfour
https://www.thearielbalfour.com/
https://www.trauma2triumphcoachinginc.com/

Ariel Balfour is an Emotional Wellness Warrior who helps burnt out, struggling to thrive people get off the emotional roller coaster of life and take charge of their own destiny.

She removes the stigma of therapy, giving tools they need to free themselves so they can build a life of fulfillment, happiness, and freedom.

After years of struggling to uncover the root causes of some of her own hot mess tendencies, she recognized the role that trauma plays in everyone's life, and decided it was time to do something about it.

Her work combines rRest, EFT Tapping, Kundalini and holistic life coaching, so you can take charge and create a life of authenticity, intentionality, and free from the internal chaos trauma leaves us with. Ariel is revolutionizing the way we view and heal Mental Health and Trauma, are you ready to become the warrior of your destiny?

Living Takes Courage

By Ariel Balfour

Dying was easy... It was living that took courage.

No one can prepare you for death. People of various backgrounds and religious beliefs speculate on what they believe to be true. For me, I didn't know what my beliefs were. On one hand, I had learned from a young age that God would not accept me and that I was the only one I could rely on. For me, death looked like watching from a distance, willing myself back to my body. Each time knowing I was meant to be here and my time was not done. It took me three times to finally accept my mission on this earth. Three times I had to learn, and learning is not so easy. With each time, the lesson got deeper.

The first time is one that I held close to my heart for a very long time, mostly to protect my mother from worrying unnecessarily. It is also the most ingrained in my brain. The sights, sounds, pain, and people regularly haunt my dreams—a burden I wish on no one. I was young and dumb, and it was the first time I really tasted the true essence of life and its fragility.

It was a chilly spring morning, and I was away at camp helping out. It was kayak day, and I couldn't be more excited because I loved being on the water. I had no idea what to expect, but everyone was most excited for this portion of our stay, so naturally, I fed off the room's energy and began to get pumped up, too. Plus, water always spoke to my soul.

My shoes squished in the mud as I sauntered down the grassy hill to the docks, the wind whipping my face with a frigid slap. *Who goes out on a boat dressed in layers??* It felt odd to be doing a summer-style activity in almost winter-like clothes, but I continued on, refusing to let the chill in the air stop me from the adventure I was embarking on. I am always up for a new adventure.

As I took those first steps onto the dock, hearing the creaking of the wood, I breathed deeply, closing my eyes to soak in the sounds of calm before chaos. A piercing screech from one of the 5th graders abruptly pulled me out of my moment, so I turned to raise my clipboard and gather my crew. As the head leader delivered the safety precautions, I closed my eyes once more, allowing my mind to wander in perfect bliss.

"You got that, Ariel?" the camp counselor said with an aggressive eyebrow rise.

"Ya, I got it, we're good! I've done this like a million times," I lied to take the attention back off me. *URGH! Why did I say I haven't done this a million times? I haven't ever been on a kayak before, let alone know its safety features. What did he say? Use your paddles if you flip, pull yourself out? God dammit, Ariel, this is why you always struggle to pay attention, stupid ADHD. Oh well, we will figure it out, how hard can it be anyway?* The gravity of that final thought still weighs heavy on my heart because I learned it was, in fact, VERY hard.

At first, I took to the activity with ease and grace, the martial arts background had given me the perfect tools for balance. As the group continued on taking in the surroundings of the lake, it was like being in a faraway land of perfection. I gazed longingly at the forest line taking in every moment, when the flash of a huge bass caught my eye. I leaned over to try and see his beauty when I felt my center balance tipping me over, plunging headfirst into the icy water.

SPLASH—My paddle releases from my hands as I flail beneath.

FUCK! I GOTTA GET OUT! I struggled to push myself away from the boat only to realize my pants were stuck, and I was quickly running out of breath. Death is easy, drowning is terrifyingly easy. After the panic reaches max and you realize you can't fight anymore, it becomes eerily blissful. I felt my soul separate from my physical body, it was as if I was meant to feel no pain at all but to learn from the picture I saw before me.

That's when the surrender came, but as quickly as that set in, my body was being violently ripped from the boat and the water and, with it, my soul.

I watched separated as chest compressions started, in awe that such a scrawny man could have so much strength. As I prayed for his hard work to pay off, I felt a tug as I got pulled back into my body. Like with a rope tied around my waist, I was dragged with painful strength back to my dying body. I came to and gasped for air, sputtering out the water that filled my throat.

Living felt harder at that moment, the searing pain in my chest a reminder of how fragile I truly was. The spasming of my muscles and the fear that enveloped me all came crashing in around me as the panic and realization kicked in. Death had knocked at my door and had knocked hard. As I tried to gain my bearings, I heard a whisper in the wind, "You are meant for more."

The essential lesson was this: Ignorance and self-importance are no substitutes for true knowledge and the humility to keep learning. Genuine listening and presence are not just virtues—they are lifelines to a meaningful life.

It was years before I would need another lesson (it was my 21st birthday, to be exact). For years, I had felt superior since that first fateful day that I had cheated death. I reveled in my amazing ability to beat the odds, claiming full responsibility for my success in coming back, all the while keeping it hidden from those who mattered most. How naive and selfish I was, and I didn't even know it at the time. I took up smoking because I believed asthma and drowning had no hold on me; I beat the odds, and I was unstoppable. Then, the lesson came as it always does, in perfect timing with the perfect misstep.

It was chilly on that October 2nd day as I approached my university, dreading the math class I was about to attend and resenting the fact that, as an adult, I was still expected to do things on my birthday. I was cranky and tired and didn't care who knew it, this had been a lingering feeling for months. I felt off and was unsure why. As I looked up the wide staircase leading up to my class, I let out an irritated sigh knowing those two flights of stairs were going to be the worst ever because I had convinced myself of it. I took my first few heavy-footed angsty steps feeling my chest tighten already. Having asthma plus cold, wet weather was no joke, but I stomped on as if I were on the march of my life. Little did I know that I was.

As I reached the second-floor landing, there was a sharp and painful stab in my chest, the feeling of a burning knife slicing into me, my lungs filling with hot fluid, and a sense of drawing on air consumed me. It was unbearable as I tried to take breath after breath with little success, shaking as I felt the familiar pull away. The world began to sink into darkness—pure darkness, an abyss of loneliness. There were no moments to watch, no pain or fear, just conscious darkness and a feeling of being out of my body.

You always hear about the light that people see when they die, in my case, it was the light coming back into my body and the blinding fluorescent hospital lights. The alarms from all of the machinery were deafening and all-consuming. The pain was insurmountable.

What felt like moments in and out of conversations were months, everything blurring into one moment after the next. By this point, for the first time in my life, I had to seriously contemplate my mortality and the meaning of life—my life. This is not a subject many people consider at length. By this time, I had tested my fate twice, so a deep reflection was needed.

"Recovery is not glamorous, nor will it be easy," the doctor said in a stern voice as he glared over the top of his glasses. "You are not invincible, and your choices have been reckless at best." He, of course, was referring to the fact that I had taken to smoking a pack a day, feeling the devil on my shoulder pushing me to test the limits.

I knew it was dumb, hell, I didn't even like the taste of ashtray in my mouth or nights I struggled to breathe, but doing so, I felt like a rebel testing the fates of the gods, if there even was one. Up until this point, I didn't give a fuck about anyone's opinion of me or my life. After all, I was the one having to live it. As I listened and looked through weary eyes, I could see the fear on my mother's face and the concerned disappointment on my stepfather's, both triggering a feeling of shame and guilt, catapulting me straight into defensiveness.

"I do what I want!" I said with such defiance, it immediately created a fight there in that tiny sterile room. The details of the argument are cloudy in the drug-induced mind scrambling for clarity, but I suppose those words exchanged were never the point.

What felt like an eternity to breathe normally in reality only took maybe 2 years of intense rehab, but in that time, deep realizations had to be acknowledged and healed. I was *NOT* invincible, and my careless behavior was a reflection of the battle I was waging against myself from within. The battles I had long ignored, that I covered with rage and rebellion instead of care and empathy; the battle with my internal demons. Living takes courage, facing what you choose to repress takes balls. This death was truly a rebirth as I donned myself with warrior armor and prepared to go to war. A war fought for the ultimate prize—internal peace.

This moment in time taught me that the universe is always guiding us, teaching us valuable lessons to ensure we are ready for what is to come next. I learned at that moment to listen to the whispers of the universe and to face the discomfort with embracing empathy. We are all just lost, little children desperately trying to find the light to save us from the dark.

I spent years confident the lessons were learned, and I was taking the right path as I had armored up to embark on my healing journey of growth and exploration of self. However, I was side-swiped by my third and most potent lesson to date. True living means surrendering to what is meant for you.

Surrender was never a word I resonated with. I viewed it as a sign of weakness, something I most definitely was not. I had no idea that surrender had so many beautiful complexities that could lead a soul down so many portals of possibility. I was a warrior, after all, and not meant to surrender but rather to fight my way to the outcomes I desired. But as I had learned in depth by this point, dying was easy, it was the living that took bravado and courage.

My warrior status by 2013 had been well-established, creating a name for myself in the world of MMA. I had proven my worth time and time again. First, by going against everything that felt safe to me and stepped full-on into a sport that was not at the time readily accepting of women but readily well on its way. You see, I had an innate infinity for fighting, my Viking blood runs deep, and my soul spoke only the language of a fighter. To this day, I hear the whispers of the war carried on the wind. Being in the octagon felt like home. It was my lifeline, my release, and yet it was also my darkest secret. Fighting was not just something I was a natural at, but there was a bloodlust for the fight, for the insatiable win.

All of that came crashing down in a moment. Double dislocation, both legs gone in an instant. It's not something you can prepare for or even begin to understand the ripple effect in full. One moment, one choice, or step in the wrong path and everything shifted. You see, by this point, I had already made up my mind that this was my path, the path of a fighter. What felt so natural to me could be the only answer. However, for years, I heard and equally ignored the whisper of "You are made for more." What more could there be? I had chosen my path to go professional or to become an officer to protect those who could not protect themselves, but at that one moment, the timeline shattered into infinite possibilities.

As I sat irritated in the hospital bed, pain echoing its way through my body, I began to calculate what the outcome may be. One miscalculation in the ring had left me bound and broken on the floor, screams echoing in the rafters, eyes blurred with agony and sorrow. I snapped back to the moment as I eyed the doctor with disdain as he made an annoying clicking sound with mild grunting noises while reviewing my scans and file.

"Well, looks like surgery is the only option, Ms. Sommers, you did quite the number on yourself. I'm glad your mother is here visiting, as this will be quite the road to recovery and not one I can assure you will lead to any outcome you desire, but let's see what the surgeon says, shall we?" He flips the pages down as he forces that tight-lipped smile, the one that screams how much he hates delivering bad news. The next few hours getting more testing done, and seeing the surgeon all confirmed one certainty, which was that reconstruction of the ACL, MCL, and Meniscus was unavoidable in both legs. The problem was that normally they would fix one and rehab it before touching the next, but both were in such a shape that Bilateral reconstruction with deep physio was our only option. The new and overgrown path emerged, shrouded in mystery.

I remember thinking to myself as I counted back from 10 how much I couldn't wait to be done. Wrong wording. The shrieking sirens and beeps from hospital machinery were going off, crushing my skull with its shrillness. As I saw myself lying there, my heart rate stopped, and I realized at once the all too familiar separation from self. *FUCK FUCK FUCK, NOOOO, NOT AGAIN.* As I watched with feverish eyes, I was captivated by the movement in the room. Doctors and nurses moved with the ease of a dance partner, each predicting what the next needed and countered to perfection. It was mesmerizing. I bore my eyes into my own skull, willing myself back to my vessel. *I AM NOT DONE HERE DAMMIT, NOT YET.* The sounds echoing in my ears began to fade as I focused all of my energy back towards my being.

SNAP The all too familiar tug back into my body. *PHEW*. Then, the agony hit, as I heard a voice, "...her pain is not being controlled, her heart rate is spiking fast, but we can't deliver more meds without crashing her again..." Then, darkness hit. A floating sensation and voices in the distance with a faint undertone of pain kept me drifting in and out of my mind as I continued to float.

The light from the morning sun warmed my face as I opened my eyes to another day. A tear escaped the corner of my eye as gratitude washed over me. The pain was a reminder that I was alive and not something I wanted to take for granted again. As I watched the sunrise I asked an important question to the universe. *WHAT NOW?* I lay there for what felt like an eternity, drawing out the background noise, tuned into the frequency of the earth until I heard that soothing, familiar voice... "You are made for more." I breathed it so deeply into my soul, only to answer with one word: *YES*.

You see, the lesson this round was that you can't outrun your demons or fight your way out of dealing with the true depths of your soul because it is within those dark depths that you find your true strength and most vibrant light. By shining that light in the cavern of my soul, I found myself, my true self. She is magnificent and has always been a part of me, but I had been conditioned and taught to hide her away. My battles were not against myself to see me fail but rather to see me rise to my fullest potential. The cosmos was there to get back in alignment for every misstep off my guided path. For every word whispered in anger and resentment, they covered it in love and understanding. Living takes courage, and trust falling into the arms of something greater than myself was natural.

I am a warrior. I am a leader. I am love. I am peace. I WAS MADE FOR MORE.

Emily Cleghorn

Mamahood After Trauma
Trigger Recovery Coach

www.linkedin.com/in/emily-cleghorn-149933201
https://www.facebook.com/mendedsoullife
https://www.instagram.com/emily.mamahoodaftertrauma/
https://mamahoodaftertrauma.ca/mended-mama-heart-to-heart
https://mamahoodaftertrauma.ca/mat-subscriber

Emily Cleghorn is an award-winning Trigger Recovery Coach, author, and inspirational speaker, passionate about helping trauma-surviving mamas reclaim peace in their lives. With firsthand experience navigating triggers and emotional overwhelm, Emily understands the challenges of healing childhood trauma while parenting. Through her Mended Mama Method and as the host of Mamahood After Trauma, Emily provides mothers with transformative tools to manage triggers, foster resilience, and break generational cycles of trauma. Her mission is to empower mamas to build lasting emotional strength and create a nurturing, stable environment for their children. Emily's unique approach combines practical techniques with compassion, offering mamas a supportive pathway to self-healing and emotional recovery. Emily lives in New Brunswick with her husband and two children, where she is dedicated to creating ripples of hope and healing for generations to come.

The Trauma Freight Train

By Emily Cleghorn

September 3, 2018—the day my life changed forever. It was a day that I didn't dream about as a little girl. I didn't expect it to happen like many other girls do. In fact, until I met my husband, it was completely out of the question—a decision I had made at fourteen or fifteen years old. I had made the decision to not want kids in my teens out of fear.

I was afraid of recreating the childhood I had experienced for another generation, and that wasn't something I wished on anyone. Have you felt that fear? It consumed me for such a long time, but what I have come to understand is that I—we—are not confined by that fear. We can break free from that fear, and it doesn't have to hold me, or you, back.

I was the little girl no one wanted. Abandoned by my biological mother at 7 months old, abused by my stepfamily between the ages of 6 and 7 years old, and invisible the rest of the time. In my limited experience, mothers were unsafe and gave conditional love, which was to be earned. However, I knew at a very young age that my experience and the experience of many other little kids who had parents who didn't know how to love them, wasn't normal, and there, a fire ignited in my soul to someday, somehow help these kids like me.

I had spent much of my teens and early 20s running away from the cloud that trauma covered me with. I was sick of the emotional pain following me everywhere I went and dictating how my life would go. So, I did the only thing I knew how to do—I numbed out and ran.

This worked... kind of—for a while. I mean, I still dealt with anxiety and depression, but I could stuff those just like I was stuffing everything else. This worked until other issues started coming up that were more difficult to ignore, like hormone imbalances and digestive dysfunction, which I learned to live with.

This meant that when my husband and I started trying to conceive, we had to be very intentional. Achieving a healthy pregnancy was no easy task for us. First, going the mainstream route and enduring a miscarriage. Then, shifting to a more natural, holistic route, learning how to support my body and how my past was once again wrecking havoc in my present.

This eventually led to a healthy pregnancy. Little did I know, this journey to achieving pregnancy was only the tip of the iceberg, waiting for me to heal.

The rest of the iceberg would make itself known mere days after my beautiful baby entered the world. The best way I can describe it to you is it was like a freight train came barreling down the tracks, coming straight at me and mowing me over. I was completely in love with this beautiful baby, but I was also completely overwhelmed by my survival instincts.

The internal dialogue happening in my head was so conflicting.

"I love her so much."

"I hate being a mom, and I can't tell anyone because they'll think I'm an awful person, mother and wife."

"She's so beautiful."

"I have to keep these feelings quiet so he doesn't leave me, and I end up alone for real."

"I love our little family."

"I need to get the hell out of here, but I can't leave because that will hurt her like I was hurt."

On one hand, I wanted to run far, far away and never look back—while on the other hand, I knew the fallout that would happen if I gave way to the survival instinct that was screaming at me—I would repeat the maternal abandonment that I had experienced 27 years prior, and that wasn't okay with me.

Day in and day out for the first 2 months of my postpartum journey was a raging war that I was battling all alone because the narrative in my head was telling me that if I let anyone see this part of me, they would judge me as the awful person, wife and mother I was and I would be alone—abandoned once again.

Until I couldn't hold it in any longer.

I believe it was a Saturday afternoon. My husband and I had packed up our daughter in a car seat and headed to the town about 45 minutes away to get some groceries and go to my favourite coffee shop for lunch. On our way home, I was looking out the window, trying to hide the tears streaming down my face.

My husband noticed and asked, "What's wrong?"

I shrugged him off like I had done for months at that point, not wanting to let him see this part of me. This time he wouldn't let it go. He pressed me until I got fed up and blurted it out—"I HATE BEING A MOTHER!"

The look on his face was one of shock. He didn't know what to say. I continued, "Don't get me wrong, I love our daughter more than life, but I hate being a mother."

"Okay, how do we make it better?" he asked.

"I don't know," I answered, and the rest of our drive was silent. I was shocked, honestly. I was expecting my husband to be appalled by how I was feeling (not that he had a history of reacting that way); instead, he was focused on helping me through it and supporting me.

By this point, I had already made my decision to stay and figure it out but now it was time to put my money where my mouth was and start.

The first thing I did was search for other mamas who could support me in the day-to-day, people I could talk to for company. I started finding ways to go have lunch with my co-workers. Little things that got my daughter and I out of the house and around other people.

Then, I started searching for a therapist that I could speak with. I found a lady who did sessions virtually, which helped because we lived extremely rurally. Those sessions helped me to understand my personal boundaries—where my biological mom stopped and where I started, where I stopped and where my daughter started. They also helped me to understand that I was not doomed to repeat the choices my mom made when I was a baby, and I could make my own choices—my motherhood journey was my own, and my daughter's childhood was her own.

These realizations were earthshaking for me. They lifted a weight that I could not have carried for much longer.

In the days, weeks and months that followed, I began to learn about my nervous system. I started by raising my awareness of my emotions as they were coming to the surface. This was a huge process for me because I had been an emotion stuffer for so long, and this was a process of unlearning habits that I had fine-tuned.

Understanding that my emotions were connected to various parts of my body and that my physical health was directly connected to my stress level and my emotional health. Then, I took another step forward and started the process of learning more functional coping mechanisms. I moved from being sidelined by my nervous system for days to gradually decreasing my rebound time. This process was painfully slow—especially after becoming a mama of 2 under 2; however, it was life-changing because my nervous system started to heal, and I became more functional as a human, especially as a mama and wife.

Listen, this isn't an easy path to walk—it certainly hasn't been for me. For the longest time, it felt like I wasn't making any progress at all because every time my little one had a temper tantrum or was inconsolable, my nervous system would go into overdrive. However, that didn't stop me. I was patient with myself, and then all of a sudden, one day, I was able to handle my son's temper tantrum without having one myself. It was absolutely amazing.

How did I really accomplish this? Let's take some time now to map out the specific steps that I have found to work for not only myself but also my clients, so you can also help your nervous system.

First, I had to get really curious about what the signs and symptoms were in my body that would indicate a trigger that was happening in my body. Things like breathing fast/hard, sweating, not being able to think clearly, anxiety rising, feeling unsettled or discontent, being on edge mood-wise. Simply recognizing these things happening in my body was a huge step.

Then, noticing what situations were connected to those physical symptoms as well as noticing where I was feeling them in my body. This step was also accompanied by giving myself space to allow the wave of emotions to pass and limiting the stimuli I was taking in. Early on in my journey, that looked like me pulling the hood of my sweater up and pulling the drawl strings tight to limit what I could see, covering my ears, and curling up in a ball until the intensity of the emotions was bearable. Eventually, my coping skills evolved, and I added other strategies for calming my nervous system.

There are dozens upon dozens of different calming/mindfulness strategies that serve the same purpose. For me, mindful breathing and journaling helped tremendously.

Mindful breathing was a tool that I would use when I could feel anxiety rising up in my body when I would typically hold my breath. This was challenging at first because it felt a lot like I was holding my breath even though I wasn't. This type of strategy is really effective in calming your nervous system and switching it from fight or flight to rest and digest.

Journaling has been something I've done for many years, but it wasn't until recently that I began to utilize it as a healing tool. The major benefit of journaling is that it's another way that you can get your emotions and thoughts out without talking to anyone instead of stuffing all that down into your body tissues, where it will fester and cause dysfunction and disease. So, my journaling practice is one where I allow myself to let my guard down and let everything out. Let the word flow through the pen onto the page without judgement. Sometimes reading it back to myself led to an incredibly tearful response, which is immensely cleansing, although, if that's something you're uncomfortable doing with other people around, I recommend finding a safe space where you can be alone.

As time progressed, I also added a post-trigger reflection practice where I simply asked myself about the trigger I experienced: What was the cause? How did I handle it? What (if anything) did I learn from the event? This reflection gave me many insights, and I learned a lot about my healing process and the work I had left to do.

That's where I started, and it may not sound like much, but each step is hard work when you've disassociated and fixated on external validation for the majority of your life. This process requires consistency and lots of patience because it moves snail's speed. However, it's immensely important work to do, especially if you desire to break the generational trauma cycle you fell victim to. Until your nervous system feels safe and is no longer in anticipation of fight or flight, healing the trauma will be an uphill battle because it will impact every aspect of your life in a negative way, with or without you recognizing it, due to the beliefs you are walking through life with.

The trauma you and I experienced as children was not our fault and was completely out of our control. However, our healing is within our control, and it's our responsibility to do the work.

Elizabeth Reece

Quiet Waters Coaching & Consultancy
Positive Psychology & Coaching Interventionalist

https://www.linkedin.com/in/elizabeth-reece-msc-appcp-26357a14/
https://www.facebook.com/elizabethreece.coaching/
https://www.instagram.com/seeking_quietwaters/
https://www.quietwaters.space
https://quietwatersrettreats.com

Elizabeth Reece's debut novel is a commentary on the dark side of positive psychology. With a twenty-five-year career as a workplace consultant, she was chiefly concerned with the delivery of high performance corporate environments.

Coming into sobriety and recovery from alcohol and her own workplace challenges, she found herself horrified by the lip service being paid to creation of psychologically safe spaces. She is fascinated by the cages created by our environments and relationships and the traps our mind sets for us, making escape seem impossible.

Requalifying with a Masters in Applied Positive Psychology and Coaching Psychology, she is primarily interested in the spiritual growth found in the journey through suffering to flourishing.

Recovery showed her what a true psychologically safe space could look like and as the world continued to turn and people continued to behave in untreated ways, she realized that the responsibility to create our own psychologically safe space, lies within us all.

Today she helps woman grow through their recovery. Applying principles from Positive Psychology theories of self-determination, 12-step programs and therapeutic modalities, to flourish without fear, no matter what life throws at them.

Decades of experience and observation have been poured into the narrative with the abundant hope that she has lived the research, so that other women won't have to. The patterns are clear and ignoring them brings forth the demon of chaos.

She resides in France with her Egyptian street dog, Jonnie (Female) Coaching online and in person, leveraging local businesses with beautiful venues for retreats for woman looking to find themselves again in the quiet.

The Tricks of Trauma Bonding

By Elizabeth Reece

He could have ended her life.

No one would ever have known what he did or how he did it. It unfolded so quickly and covertly that no one would have believed that it was not her who was sick, or incompetent, or indeed, the abuser.

In truth, she would come to realise, it was not so fast after all. She was made the mark of a man who was dug in for the long con. He had her in his sights for decades. She had conducted her adult life, blissfully unaware that she was being stalked. Studied and groomed. A friendship she held dear, cultivated from their early teens, with a façade of superficial charm that would serve to misdirect and mislead her as she placed her trust in a master manipulator with a lifetime of dark secrets that were shortly to come to light.

She stood, trembling in the half-light. It had been the most terrifying five hours of her life, being driven around in circles with no idea where she was going to end up.

She watched him stride away from the car. She watched intently, lest he should turn, and she would have to stand her ground. She stood still for what seemed an age, eyeing the space where his rage had been before he disappeared around the corner of the old church, towards the apartment he had shared with her. Before he went away, he had wrestled from her the keys to her only home and abandoned her.

Her rucksack at her feet, she checked her phone. He had laughed in her face when she pleaded to let her charge it. Five percent. Bastard, she smirked. It was so petty, so childish and malicious that it was ridiculous. She must not minimize or humourise anymore. Neglecting to recognise abuse in her story was part of the problem. She just hadn't got that far in her voyage of self-discovery, yet.

She wondered if it might have held out longer if she hadn't been recording him. It didn't matter. She had only recently taken to recording snippets of conversation here and there to refer to as evidence to maintain her sanity. She hadn't considered that anyone else might find them and use them as evidence.

Her mind raced, but she felt strangely calm. She glanced at her surroundings. She was in a tiny village in the middle of nowhere in Eastern France. Surrounded by mountains and gorges, wild and majestic landscapes. Beautiful for long hikes, yet unappealing for sleeping rough. Limited public transport and accommodation. One hotel, in fact, that had remained firmly locked as she had beaten on the door and rung the bell incessantly the night before, had been closed all year.

She needed to move. It was getting dark, and she had to decide how to use her precious five percent of battery. She had no internet connection as he had managed to ensure that she must tether to his phone and would not make the time to get her, her own independent contract. She had relied on him for so much! She couldn't yet speak French and was met with criticism and disdain when she tried.

She had read about women who were trapped in their controlling relationships, and it was only now she could see how easily it could happen. How she had created a more romantic notion of her predicament, when it was, in fact, a carefully cultivated cage. When he asked, "Do you think I brought you here to trap you?" She now knew the answer was "Yes."

But she wasn't trapped now. She knew her future was going to be held to ransom, but right then, she was OK.

She shouldered her hastily packed bag and made her way to the hotel. Miraculously, it was open! There was a pilgrimage taking place and they were full. She secured the last available room for the night.

She awoke on June 1st, 2023, to glorious sunshine and feeling lighter than she had in months. As she dressed for the day, the 'skinny girl' shorts that had fit her snugly, now hung off her hips as she considered the challenges around food in the household she had just been evicted from. She had all but disappeared, and no one had noticed or cared.

A year on, she would come to know it as World Narcissistic Abuse Awareness Day. She did not know it then, but she did believe that she had just escaped the clutches of an abusive narcissist, ASD, BPD – she hadn't worked it all out yet. Abuse is abuse, and all abuse is narcissistic. She knew enough to know with certainty that she had been cruelly and dispassionately treated and deceived. She was no longer confused. Looking for her part, she had escaped a dangerous individual who could not recognise physical abuse as a moral and legal crime and whose gaslighting had minimized every aspect of the emotional and psychological abuse perpetrated in the months preceding his eventual meltdown.

She had friends. She was not alone in this. Despite what he told her. In the gap between the attack and the abandonment, she had received phone calls from friends all over the world. It was as if an invisible bat signal had gone up and been answered. She was told to get out immediately. Leave everything. Figure it out later. Get to an airport and fly to Johannesburg, Portugal, or back to London.

She was scared to leave. She didn't know where to go or what to do. Who to tell. As her story unfolded, she would realise just how lucky she was. He had tried to trap her. He had tried to coerce her into harebrained financial schemes. She had seen the insanity and kept her money separate. She had never disconnected from her world. She had only dabbled in the shared fantasy. She had not lost herself to the relationship and in servitude of that man with the broken brain and maniacal ego.

She boarded a bus, deciding to take each day as it came and treat the experience like a season of *Survivor*. An adventure. She had everything she needed to survive.

There is a shelf life for survival mode in a human being, and the time would soon come when her life would depend, again, on getting herself out of it.

The ensuing six months became a series of wonderful blessings and torturous psychological battles. Caught somewhere between a bizarrely liberating spiritual retreat and a mental prison with no bars, she existed. Sometimes in deep joy and gratitude and others in great fear and anxiety.

She was not lonely. She made her way to her house. A derelict and uninhabitable farmhouse in a tiny hamlet near the Saone River. A project they had taken on in partnership. One, she had gladly ploughed almost everything she had left to show for a thirty-year career and a lifetime of grafting in London. She was still hopeful that she could create something magical there. The safe space that she had craved. For others like her to gather, write, cook, enjoy the garden, marvel at the clear nights and delight in each other's company.

She felt strongly that she needed to be there. That it could be her safe space. The sellers had left her a Caravan. A 1991 Alouette in pristine condition. A stroke of good fortune as they had demolished every wall in the house and ripped up the uneven terracotta tiled floors, leaving only a cold and dusty shell, damp, cold and a haven for spiders and swallows.

She was mentally prepared to make that Caravan her home for the Summer. Perhaps jumping in her newly acquired but ancient Peugeot Partner van, hastily purchased in desperation, to jaunt around France and Italy as the weather cooled into autumn. She was daydreaming. Escaping. She had very real and urgent matters to attend to. On a precarious Entrepreneur Visa for one year – how on earth could she be expected to work, let alone earn money? She must validate her visa and secure her first year. She could not return to the UK. She had cut those kite strings. She had precious little financial resources and no one in her family to offer comfort of any kind. She was alone.

She was smart. Capable and resourceful, and most importantly, she was sober.

He had looked on impassively as she expressed concerns about her drinking thoughts within two weeks of her arrival. Nearly five years sober, she knew beyond a shadow of a doubt that the gaslighting was shaking her sanity. The confusion was causing her brain to search for answers and comfort. The isolation and proximity to the cause of the problem expedited and amplified it, sending her out into the mountains for twice-daily rides and into many new Zoom meetings.

Several months later, when suicide seemed preferable to living with that kind of fear and confusion and knowing that she had chosen to live, time and time again, she surveyed the stony dispassionate face as he listened to her pleas and concerns. She knew her mind. She understood her thoughts. She was not controlled by them but they were being manipulated and twisted, as someone else took up residence in her head. Sucking and draining the life out of her.

Each expression of emotion met with hostility and disdain. She was alone.

She came to France to write, coach and cook. To be part of something wholesome and liberating. Powerfully useful to others, and now she must take all that learning and apply it in her own life.

There were many red flags. She spotted them all. She called them out. She discussed them. The problem was that what few boundaries she had were weak. Attachments are complicated, and despite being a recovering 'love avoidant' with a Secure Attachment Style, her longest-standing and most deeply buried limiting belief was showing up in her reality, and her armour was too weak to protect her from that evil. At least, it was too weak not to let it in and give it access to every aspect of who she was. Every dream, fear, insecurity, and to entrust it with her future.

In January 2023, they were working at her house in Gigny-sur-Saone. Smashing down walls and clearing out rubble. The relationship had not enjoyed any kind of honeymoon period. She felt like an annoying house guest. The devaluing began the moment she arrived.

You can't keep a good Leo down, though, and so she applied hope, optimism, humour and kindness to the challenges that she did not yet see for what they really were. Months of textbook psychological, emotional and, ultimately, physical abuse ensued. The purpose of this story is to address how she arrived in that situation, and her predicament became very clear during that cold and frosty day at her house when part of her still hoped that everything she had come to France for was still a possibility.

She thought it would be fun to write their limiting beliefs on the last of the walls before they smashed them to dust. Symbolic of a fresh start and a bright future. She went first, or they would still be waiting by that wall.

She wrote, 'I don't deserve the things I want and desire.' She hesitated after 'deserve'... She was conflicted. She was thinking, 'I don't deserve any of this.' This person, this future, this life. It seemed as if everything had finally aligned, and she would not go through the rest of her life, fulfilling her dreams alone. What she wanted to write was, 'I don't deserve love.' That was the overarching voice in her head. She didn't feel safe enough to articulate that.

It just didn't make sense. Happy, confident, doing all the right things. No outward signs that she was lacking in self-love, self-determination, or self-worth or that she would find her dreams turn to nightmares so quickly.

On the surface, she could kid herself that she didn't know where the belief had come from when she was standing next to a man, in a house that could have been their future life and business. But she knew where it had come from and had an idea that the bleak and chilling

She Defies | 169

environment, the rubble and wreckage she was standing in, all meant something. She was becoming aware and could see how willingly she had walked into the trap made just for someone like her.

She walked into the trap willingly. The ultimate act of self-sabotage. To be so blinkered to her truth that she could see, hear and feel them, yet still ignore all the red flags.

She spent six months in her very own version of a spiritual retreat. Sometimes in heaven, and paradoxically it felt like a psychological hell as she used all the tools at her disposal to work on her house and in her garden, to heal her soul and her spirit.

She enjoyed figs, cherries and apples from the trees. She grew tomatoes and chilies and was delighted as her little vegetable patch sprung to life. She showered outside, using a solar shower during that time, driving ten minutes to the nearest town to use the public facilities when she needed a toilet or had to do the laundry. It was a strange, inconvenient and yet incredibly satisfying existence.

She charmed her neighbours with her Franglais and benefited from their unconditional friendship and kindness. She wanted them to know that she wasn't crazy. This was not how she had expected to live. It didn't matter to them. They brought her a desk to work at, tomatoes, pumpkins and squash from their own gardens. They mowed her vast, uneven lawn and seemed to arrive when she was at her lowest ebb to pass the time and make sure she was OK.

She spent hours outside, trying to tidy up her land. She was beginning to see how naïve she had been. Her own dreams had blinded her to the reality and enormity of the task, irrespective of the deception.

He maintained a stranglehold over her progress, and it was driving her insane. She needed to break free from his presence and from the thought traps that had been laid. With his abusive nature and penchant for embittered tales of victimhood, she had realized that she was not the first and would not be the last.

Applying the same logic to her predicament, she needed him to be the last! So much potential is unfulfilled by the oppression of the conditioning by others. He was not the first but she knew who was. She knew where it had begun, and she had tried her whole life not to have to look back at this. Now, she had no choice. These types of people would keep showing up as they had done repeatedly in her intimate relationships, and in her work life, if she didn't stare down her greatest fear and banish it once and for all.

She understood everything she needed to know about these personality types. The havoc and destruction they cause. She had been gently guided to understand her part in her relationship with her abusive and neglectful parents. It is widely understood that the most definitive symptom of unhealed childhood trauma is trying repeatedly to get people who treat someone appallingly to treat them better. She must shift the focus to herself and her wellbeing and her future, only.

It was so baked into her way of being. Like a cat that wraps itself around the one person in the room who hates cats, but unlike the cat, the human is an emotional being who can be hurt time and time again as they struggle to understand why the mistreatment persists.

She tracked back painfully through her past. Having worked a twelve-step program to the best of her ability, she could see it had been incredibly effective in transforming her outlook. The problem of alcohol was no longer an issue. To get sober, the 'why?' a person drinks is a distraction from the work itself. Things become much clearer the further away they get from their last drink.

The 'why?' does not go away. It just waits until they are ready to look at it. She thought that her 'why?' wasn't big or important enough to worry about, and yet, here it was threatening to destroy her life. Possibly even kill her.

She looked at every friendship, intimate relationship, toxic workplace and family estrangement as the patterns clearly emerged. Stockholm Syndrome, Cognitive Dissonance, Cult-like mentality and brainwashing. She had been conditioned for tolerance and silence. She knew now that secrets had kept her sick. How else had she ended up in yet another cycle of abuse with another victim of his own generational trauma and maladaptive coping mechanisms?

She wondered at her own pathology, as many in her situation are wont to do. Concluding that never in her darkest moments could she contrive to visit upon others what had been visited upon her. In childhood, in relationships and in her workplaces. For whatever reason, her development had gone one way while others were now irreparably dangerous.

She realized that she had been training for this. She had focused on helping others break their patterns and had not been thorough in recognizing her own. Circumstances then conspired to create a situation that was so extreme, she had no choice but to look. To stare it down and to face it. She showed herself time and time again over the next year that she was capable, resourceful and abundantly loveable.

When the time came to rescue herself, she did. Because there was no one better equipped to do it. Guided, supported and loved, she learnt to trust herself and her instincts, and she inevitably found her people and her place in the warmth of the South.

Free in France to write, coach, cook, dream and feel without fear.

The Patterns & Chaos of UNTREATED Minds is out in March 2025.

Angela Leapua

Lifestyles in Harmony
Holistic Health and Business Coach

https://www.linkedin.com/in/angelaleapua/
https://www.facebook.com/angelaleapua
https://www.instagram.com/angelaleapua
https://lifestylesinharmonycoaching.com/
http://beachybohoboutique.com/

Angela Leapua, M.B.A., M.Ed., NBHWC, MSCSIA, is a Wall Street Journal and Amazon bestselling author, freelance writer, college professor, speaker, transformational leader and holistic health coach. With over 20 years in higher education, several accredited certifications including a health coach certification from IIN, she specializes in Ayurveda, functional medicine, nutrition, mindset modalities and corporate business coaching. Her diverse background enables her to thrive in corporate, group, and personal coaching.

Angela's mission is to inspire positive transformational change. Her guidance helps individuals navigate life's transitions by promoting balance and harmony in the mind, body, and soul. She believes that everyone has the potential to raise their frequency by visualizing, manifesting, and actively working toward their goals.

Whether attending one of her lectures or courses, exploring her books, or visiting her health boutique, you'll discover that Angela embraces a natural, soul-centered, and stress-free lifestyle, inspiring others to live with purpose and harmony.

A Journey of Resilience

By Angela Leapua

A Journey of Resilience

Wow, congratulations! I am beyond excited for you because you are about to read the words that will guide you through the toughest moments and help you defy any obstacle in your life. So, take a moment, pause, breathe deeply, and say these words to yourself:

> *"I am everything. I am all that I need. I am strong. I am fearless. I am loved. I am capable. I am resourceful.* There is nothing I cannot do or achieve. Every challenge, every obstacle, every chaotic moment that life throws my way, I have everything within me to overcome it. All I need to do is dig deep, tap into my inner strength, and let it rise up to guide me. I have the power to shine through any storm, to protect myself from all that surrounds me. God is within me, walking with me every second, every minute, every moment. I am filled with power and courage, because I am enough. I love myself. I love my life and no matter what comes my way, I will power through, just me, myself, and I."

These words I have spoken many times. They have gotten me through the worst of times. I have dug deep into the very core of my soul, with every ounce of strength I had, to get through the darkest moments of my own life. I faced sorrow, heartache, pain, and struggles that seemed impossible to bear. I walked through it all alone, but I made it. If I can do it, so can you.

We all have this inner strength. It's always been there, waiting for the right moment to rise up. It's in your deepest core, and you don't always realize it until life challenges you in ways you never expected. But trust me: it's there. Embrace it. Know it's within you, and when the time comes, use it. You are stronger than you think.

My Life's Tale of Challenges

As a woman who has endured life's most unimaginable challenges, I stand before you today as a testament to the resilience of the human spirit. My name is Angela Leapua, and my story is one of struggle, survival, and ultimately, triumph. This chapter is my story, but it's also the story of every woman who has been pushed down and told she couldn't rise. You *can* rise. I'm living proof.

Growing up in the heart of Indiana, I was the oldest of six children in a family close to poverty and hardship. We had no silver spoon, no inherited wealth, and no easy path to follow. My journey has not been defined by luxury, but by sheer determination and the relentless desire to create a better life for myself and my family.

When I was a child, my parents were my role models. They were a young couple full of hope and love. Having their first child (me), right out of high school, they did the best they could with what they had. My father was awarded scholarships for college and had a promising future. We lived on a college campus as both parents attended school and started to grow a family. After my father graduated college, he was diagnosed with Schizophrenia. Unfortunately, when I was 15, I lost my father, and 10 years later, my mother passed away as well. I felt like I was orphaned at an age when most are still sheltered by their parents' love and protection, I was forced to grow up quickly. Death to me seemed normal. During 6th through 10th grade, I lost my father, grandparents, younger brother, and a few friends. Attending funerals kept me numb to the pain of loss. I did not cry when death was near, I went into a state of survival and protection. Feeling sorrow but holding in the emotional pain.

After my mother passed away, I found myself feeling responsible for my younger siblings and the endless fight for freedom from my abusive stepfather. My stepfather was extremely abusive, and our mother somewhat protected us. With her passing, I took on the mother role. I thought we could start a new life without my stepfather, but that did not happen. I could not afford a lawyer, and there was no help from family or friends. Therefore, my stepfather took control of the property, my mother's family business, and, worst of all, custody of three younger siblings. I was forced to live on my own and became distant from my family. I was truly on my own. At age 25, I was dealing with my mother's death, grappling with the emotional and physical abuse, giving up control to my abuser, and losing home and family. I was at a crossroads. I was experiencing a life of turmoil, pain, and uncertainty.

Living without guidance or safety, I knew the harsh reality of fighting for survival. The weight of responsibility on my young shoulders was immense. As the oldest, I had to set an example, take charge, and bear the emotional burden of our circumstances. I had to grow up faster than I should have. But despite the overwhelming odds stacked against me, I refused to be a victim of my circumstances. There was no way I was going to fail! My stepfather degraded, belittled, and beat me black and blue. There was no way I was going to prove him right in thinking I was a waste of life and would fail. I pushed through the dark moments, determined that one day, I would rise above the limitations of my environment.

Throughout my teenage years, I sought solace in education, a lifeline that offered me hope for a future beyond the confines of my struggling home. With only a GED, little support, and no financial resources, I always thought college was out of reach for someone like me. But deep down, I knew that education was my escape, my ticket to freedom. I was the life of the party and enjoyed the social scene. This was my escape from abuse at home. Hanging out with older friends, I would stay out all night and run off to college campuses every chance I got. Little did I know that the college lifestyle would lead me to becoming a college professor. The campus was a safe haven for me. I had many friends and a sense of family; therefore, I worked part-time jobs, took out loans, or whatever it took to stay in school. Deep down, I had an unwavering belief that I could defy the odds, I earned my college degree, a milestone that felt impossible when I first set foot on that journey.

But that victory was just the beginning. The struggles I faced didn't end with my education; they only morphed into new challenges. I found myself in more abusive relationships with men who had a heart but addictive behaviors. Physical abuse, I felt I could handle it, but life with a drug addict was more challenging. I gave them excuses for their behavior and felt I could save them. After years of abuse, I literally ran for my life. This time, I ended up in a women's shelter, not a college campus. From broken bones, bruises, homelessness, stealing, guns in my face, jail time, and losing it all, I had to rebuild my life and start over again. The scars from my past—the emotional wounds from the abuse, the weight of responsibility, and the isolation—were often hard to shake. Yet, through every setback, I learned to rise. Each failure was a lesson, each hardship a step forward. With every challenge, I found new strength.

Today, as a highly accomplished woman, I stand on the other side of adversity. Through self-belief, education, and perseverance, I've become strong, resilient, and unbreakable. This chapter reflects my journey, a story of empowerment that speaks to every woman who has ever faced the darkest of days and dared to rise from them. It is a reminder that, no matter where we come from, or what we have endured, we have the power within us to shape our own destinies.

The Power of Resilience

Let's talk about resilience. It's a word we throw around a lot these days, but what does it really mean? Resilience is defined as the ability to bounce back from life's struggles and maintain psychological well-being in the face of challenges. For me, resilience was something I learned to embody simply by surviving. I didn't choose it. But as I look back, I see how I was shaped by it. When you're a child, and you're dealing with abuse, neglect, and the loss of both parents, resilience isn't a choice—it's a necessity. I had no choice but to develop it. But I also didn't realize at the time just how much strength I was building, because all I could do was push through the pain and the fear.

Every single day felt like I was running on empty. Stress and pain were suppressed, and I had to grow up fast. I was doing the best I could, but I was carrying a heavy load. I learned to take on responsibility that should have been too much for me, and in many ways, I became hardened by it. But I also learned to be resourceful, to rely on my wits, and most importantly, to trust that I could figure things out. I had no fear. I did what I needed to survive and escape the heartache.

Resilience isn't about being invincible. It's about getting knocked down and choosing to get back up, even when you feel like you don't have the strength. I remember days when I had no idea how I would make it through, but somehow, I did. Somewhere deep down, I always knew it would be ok. That positive attitude, or some might say "unrealistic thinking", kept me going.

When you're struggling to survive, you don't always have the luxury of thinking about long-term goals. But one thing I always had, even if it was buried deep beneath my fears, was hope. I believed that there was more for me out there. I believed that, somehow, things could get better. The struggle taught me how to survive, but it also gave me the strength to start building a future that would be different.

Discovering Life Purpose: From Surviving to Thriving

As a child, my purpose was simple: survive. But as I grew older, I realized that surviving wasn't enough. I didn't just want to get through life, I wanted to thrive. I wanted to find meaning beyond the pain, beyond the struggle. But how do you do that when you've never been taught what it means to have a purpose?

The search for purpose is a deeply personal one, and I didn't have a road map to follow. For me, it wasn't until I hit adulthood that I realized just how much I had been living in survival mode. I was always under stress, moving from place to place, and most days seemed chaotic. Once I got through the basics—finding stable work, securing a roof over my head—the question became: *What's next?* The hunger for something greater began to grow, and that hunger led me to continue my education.

Finding my purpose became my pursuit. I had to explore various jobs, living situations, and experiences to find my pathway to purpose. It is not easy to feel content, happy, or full of life. For most people, there is always a void and a feeling of wanting more. Purpose in life comes from identifying what you really care about, what your talents and skills are, and how you can use them to make you feel connected, needed, and happy.

I didn't have a support system that could help me navigate my future, but what I did have was a fierce determination to create something different. Education became my lifeline. I went to college not just to get a degree but because I knew it was the key to unlocking my future. There was a fire inside me that told me, *You are worth more than your circumstances. You deserve more.*

I learned that the process of learning wasn't just about academics—it was about discovering who I was. I began to explore my passions and what truly motivated me. I started to realize that I wasn't bound by my past. I didn't have to be the victim of my circumstances forever. I could create something better.

The real turning point came when I realized that education wasn't just about building a career, it was about creating a meaningful life. That life was going to be based on something deeper than just surviving. It was going to be based on purpose. My purpose became clear—not just to get an education, but to make a difference. To prove to myself and others that no matter where you come from, you have the power to create the life you deserve.

Overcoming the Past and Achieving Happiness

I have realized that success doesn't automatically bring happiness. For years, I thought that if I could just get a good job, get out of poverty, and achieve some level of success, I would finally be happy. But I quickly learned that happiness isn't something you can chase by looking at external achievements. Happiness, I discovered, is an inside job.

I spent a lot of time thinking that happiness would just appear once I crossed certain milestones off my list—graduating from college, getting a "good" job, finding financial stability. But once I ticked off all those boxes, I still felt a void. That's when I realized that the key to happiness wasn't tied to external markers of success—it was tied to the way I viewed myself, my past, and my potential.

I was still carrying the weight of my past. The emotional wounds from the abuse, the lack of feeling loved, the pain of losing my parents, and the trauma of growing up without support—it was all still there. But something shifted in me. I realized that if I was ever going to truly be happy, I had to let go of the past. Not forget it but release it. I had to forgive—not others, but myself. Letting go of anger, regrets, shame, and guilt allowed me to free myself and find inner peace.

As I healed, I began to build a life that reflected who I truly was—not the broken girl from Indiana, but the strong, independent woman I had become. I found joy in simple things: exercise, spending time by the ocean, and taking care of my body. These activities became my tools for maintaining balance and peace in my life. The ocean became a sanctuary for me—its vastness reminded me that life, like the sea, is full of ebbs and flows. The ups and downs are all part of the journey.

True happiness doesn't come from accumulating wealth or recognition. It comes from knowing that you are at peace with yourself. It comes from the freedom of letting go of the past and living fully in the present. It comes from understanding that you are enough, just as you are. And let me tell you, the more I embraced this mindset, the more happiness and fulfillment I found.

The Role of Self-Belief and Empowerment

One of the biggest lessons I've learned on my journey is the power of self-belief. For years, I allowed my past to convince me that I wasn't worthy of happiness or success. It was subconscious. I verbally told myself I was worthy, and I deserved it all. But deep down, my soul was ill with lies. It was hurt and filled with sadness. I had to take a really good look at my mindset and true self-belief. I stopped looking to others for validation. I learned that true empowerment comes from within, not from external approval or validation.

Empowering yourself means saying "no" when necessary. It means setting boundaries with people who drain your energy and protecting your peace. It means taking care of your physical, mental, and emotional health. I've learned to prioritize my well-being—not out of selfishness, but because I understand that I cannot pour from an empty cup. I started putting myself first and not others. I realized that self-care isn't just about pampering yourself—it's about taking responsibility for your own happiness and well-being.

As I grew in confidence, I realized something important: Believing in yourself doesn't mean you won't face doubts or setbacks along the way. It means you'll keep going, even when those doubts arise. Perseverance is what makes self-belief so powerful. It doesn't require perfection; it just requires the decision to keep going.

Today, I used my experiences to empower others. Empowering others is one of the most fulfilling parts of my journey. When you help someone else rise, you rise too. The act of sharing your knowledge and supporting others creates a ripple effect that can reach far beyond what we can imagine. When women support each other, we create a community that thrives. By embracing our own power and helping others to do the same, we change the world.

Conclusion: The Triumph of Resilience, Purpose, and Happiness

Looking back on my journey, I realize just how far I've come. I went from a girl who had nothing but a broken home and shattered dreams to a woman who knows her worth and her purpose. I've learned that resilience, purpose, and happiness are not destinations—they are practices. They are ways of living that we choose every day.

If there's one thing I want you to take away from my story, it's this: You have the power to change your life. No matter what you've been through, no matter where you've come from, you can create the life you deserve. It starts with believing in yourself, finding your purpose, and embracing your own strength. You've got this. If I can do it, so can you.

Jane Bromley

Stressed 2 Loving Life
Health Coach

https://www.facebook.com/jane.bromley.90
https://www.instagram.com/janebromleynomad/
https://www.linkedin.com/in/janebromley/
https://lovinglife.samcart.com/products/5-startlingly-quick-ways-to-feel-great-today
https://lovinglife.samcart.com/products/burning-out-to-thriving

An internationally renowned coach, Jane Bromley, worked in the corporate world for decades and then set up a consultancy business.

Known as the person who made things happen & solved challenging problems, she loved her work. However, the pressure was intense and, one day, her body shut down. She burnt out so badly that she was ill for years.

Eventually she healed and, now, she lives a life where she feels so alive. The chapter tells her story.

Now she guides overstressed, working mothers to thrive - healthy, energised, deeply peaceful & on top of their game. All her clients love the results they gain.

From Disastrously Burnt Out to Loving Life

By Jane Bromley

I did not know I was going to hit a wall until it happened.

Had I known the symptoms to look out for, I would have chosen so differently.

Then, the disaster would have been quite easy to avoid.

I could have saved myself years of struggle.

A Gift with Enormous Power

Have you felt overstressed and overbusy for too long? Are you determined to find a better way to live? Then, this chapter is for you.

I want to give you an incredible gift. To show you how to avoid the craziness that the Western world is suffering from and, instead, discover just how incredible each day of your life can be.

- Soak up the inspiring stories and insights
- Open up your mind to a different perspective, a great, way to live
- Answer the coaching questions to understand what loving life really means to you
- Follow some simple steps to cut your stress and begin your journey to loving life

Through this chapter, you can learn to see how to naturally become happier and who you are at your very best.

You can just read it, or you can use it to change your whole perspective so that you can start to thrive. Are you really ready to ease off the pressure, to allow your body to come back into balance? To learn to believe in yourself and your ability to enjoy each day?

I can show you the steps, but the decision is yours.

QUESTION

So, if anything was possible, what would you love to gain from this chapter?

> **82% of the Workforce is at Risk for Burnout**
>
> Forbes, April 2024

48% of employees in the US, UK, Australia, Canada, Italy, France, Germany, India, and Japan said they had burnt out in 2024. [1] Surprisingly, the percentage of people is even higher in millennials (59%) and Generation X (58%) than in older baby boomers (39%). [2]

25% more women burn out than men. [3]

Yet, I have discovered something wonderful - there is no need for anyone at all to burn out.

Once you know the pre-burnout symptoms to look for, you can make better decisions and avoid it.

I hear your doubts. Maybe you think it is out of your control? Do you believe that the only other option is to take a job that does not pay enough? That your employer or your situation gives you no choice? That prioritising your health will put your job at risk?

Those are the misconceptions I believed, too.

---

[1] Boston Consulting Group 2024
[2] BitSight January 2024
[3] BitSight January 2024.

186 | Powerful Stories of Overcoming

For now, I will just say that to thrive in this crazy Western world, you will need a new, far more empowering mindset, which will give you back control of your life. That is what I wish to give you.

BUT I am getting ahead of myself...

I got it so badly wrong that one day I did not wake up.

How Burnout Came as a Total Shock

I thought if I both worked and played hard, I would be fine. They say you should just push through. Hah! That is so stupid.

Both my hours and the pressure were too intense. It went on and on. There was just so much to do. A never-ending list. (I bet you know that feeling.)

I was running faster and faster. It became relentless.

Then, several times, clients overreacted due to stress that had nothing to do with me. One screamed down the phone at me at 11 pm, the night before I was to lead a workshop for his team. It shocked me so much that I hyperventilated.

However, I would have let 8 people down at the last minute, and I thought I needed the work. I now see that my scarcity mindset was causing me not to believe in myself. Despite his appalling behaviour, I did the workshop anyway! ☹

Although I tried to shrug them off, to just take them, these dramatic experiences shook me. The mixture of intense ongoing stress, being overbusy, and these small traumas had a deeply negative impact on my body and nervous system.

As the months went by, I started to realise that something was wrong. But I did not know the pre-burnout symptoms, so I did not see the real danger. Nor had I ever been taught to listen to my body, so I did not realise it warning me. Like most people, I thought I could just push through.

I thought I had no choice. How wrong I was.

I did make sure I was doing things for myself and playing hard, too. But, looking back on it, my nervous system was so strung up that I was in overdrive. Indeed, doing exercise 6 days a week, plus a really intense work schedule, did not even seem extreme.

One Christmas, I got off an overnight ferry crossing and decided to pull over for a half-hour nap before I drove home. I was shocked when I only woke up 4 hours later.

I should have realised then.

Instead, I behaved like an ostrich. My fear kept me stuck, and I soldiered on.

But our bodies can only take so much. A few months later, my body stopped me dead.

. . .

Yes. One morning, I just did not wake up as normal.

Instead, I slept for 16 hours.

The remaining 8 hours were a total write-off.

Actually, it was a relief. I could just let go and sleep.

But it was weeks before I even had the energy to go to the doctor.

"*I feel like a battery that can no longer recharge,*" I told him.

"*You have burnt out...*" said my doctor.

"Sadly, *there's little I can do to help. There's no tablet you can take. Go home and sleep. Walk for 15 minutes a day. No more.*"

I just let go. I collapsed back into bed and slept... and slept. It felt so good.

But then, as the days and weeks went by, I realised I was in trouble. It was frightening. I had no idea how to heal. Now, I really was stuck.

Indeed, I was so emotionally and physically exhausted that there was nothing much I could do but wait and hope.

Getting well was really difficult. The months became a year. Longer. I tried everything to heal. As the doctors could not help, I paid nutritionists, supplement companies, several alternative therapists, and everything I could find. I changed my whole way of life. And I learnt to listen to my body. But it took so, so long.

Oh, after a while, I was able to work a bit. But, then, I would have to sleep again, for days. Getting back to full energy took MUCH, MUCH longer, and it cost so much.

If only I had known the pre-burnout symptoms beforehand.

If only I had known that with a few changes, I could not only have avoided getting ill, but my performance at work and my happiness levels would have been so much better.

Please do not burn out.

Pre-Burnout Symptoms

So, if you notice any of the following symptoms, please be aware that your body is warning you that you are approaching burnout:

- You feel exhausted, like you are dragging your body around or so wired that you cannot slow down, let alone switch off
- You try so hard to hold it all together, but there is so much to do. You never seem to stop. It feels as if you are running, running all the time

- Your to-do list is controlling your life AND you!
- You notice you are forcing yourself to keep going
- However hard you try, you no longer seem to perform as well
- Your mind no longer seems as clear
- You no longer get those wonderful ahas. Your intuition seems inaccessible
- That wonderful sense of peace is elusive
- You have forgotten how to feel joy
- When you sleep, you no longer feel as refreshed
- It is hard to really wake up and harder to get out of bed
- When you wake up, you have a sinking feeling about the day ahead
- You feel anxious/on edge – even though you are not sure why
- Your muscles are tight. It's hard to relax.
- More irritable/less tolerant with others
- You overreact to situations far more than ever before
- You start to begrudge even your closest friends and loved ones your time and energy
- Deep down, you know you are not functioning as well as before

QUESTION

Which of these symptoms do you relate to? How many do you have out of the total of 18?

The list above covers the main symptoms. There are others, which differ from person to person. For example, I became very sensitive to cold. Other people develop pain. If the symptoms go on for long enough, your immune system will weaken, so you catch every single bug. You may develop mind fog where you just cannot see straight.

If you are experiencing many of the symptoms above, please hear the warning, before your body shuts down! Like a car battery that can no longer recharge. Please also show yourself a lot of compassion and kindness. It is what you need now.

Are You Avoiding Burnout but Feeling a Shadow of Your Real Self?

Even if you have not burnt out, while you feel chronic stress and are constantly too busy, your nervous system is overloaded. You are not made like a machine, to be on the go all the time. It is just not the way we are designed. So, you will notice that, however hard you try, you are no longer able to be who you are at your very best.

Let me explain.

Our nervous system is supposed to spend most of its time in parasympathetic mode. That is where life is in flow, you feel relaxed and sleep well. Where all is well with the world, little bothers you, and you naturally perform well.

However, if you have a lot of stress and you constantly push yourself too hard, you will not only go into fight or flight (the sympathetic mode), but your brain will think the danger is constant, so it will keep you there.

Therefore, your cortisol and adrenaline levels rise. You feel unable to relax the way you used to. It will not even let you sleep well because it thinks you are in danger. It keeps you feeling on edge. And it directs your blood to organs and muscles, away from your brain. So your normal access to all the ways you functioned at your best—your intuition, ability to see the big picture, to find good solutions, or to feel a deep sense of peace are all shut down.

As a result, you will feel a shadow of your former self. And, understandably, fed up.

Is It Time for You to Thrive?

Have you had enough of the constant stress and busyness yet? Enough of feeling you are just existing? Of living a half-life?

If you are sure there has to be a better way, then, you are so right.

Indeed, there are great ways to reduce your stress and literally thrive.

- To feel wonderfully full of life
- To enjoy life so much that you bounce out of bed each morning, excited about each day
- Feeling deeply at peace
- Effortlessly becoming the best version of yourself
- Seeing your performance levels naturally rise, while you feel on top of your game.

To reach this, some mindset shifts are essential:

- Being open to realising that you have never been taught how to avoid stress or support yourself to thrive
- The determination to make it work for you
- Courage to face some of your fears that have been keeping you stuck

Every single one of my clients thought they could not find time to slow down.

And every single one discovered that once they could be objective, they quickly found solutions.

What is more, every client who had prioritised their family and others above themselves, realised that, by truly living their life their way, they could give their loved ones something priceless. Once they started living life to the full, their way, their example started to literally inspire everyone around them.

> **QUESTION**
>
> **Are you ready to change how you live so you can thrive?**

Two Inspiring Case Studies

Here are the stories of two of my clients. It took courage to turn their situation around, but the result was so worthwhile.

As you read, mark the parts that resonate with you or spark ideas:

Janet – Simple Transformation

Janet had been exhausted and so fed up for so long. At the end of her tether. She was almost tearful and desperate to get out of "this nightmare job". Yet, after speaking to her for just 30 minutes, it became obvious that she:

- Said yes to almost everything anyone asked her to do, even when she had provided a simple way for them to do it themselves
- Was not making it clear how they could do many of the tasks themselves
- Was putting herself at the bottom of the priority list

After just a 1-hour conversation, she agreed to make some simple changes. As a result, her workload decreased by 30%. Within 1 week, she started to enjoy her job and her life again. She started to wake up, looking forward to each day. People noticed how much happier she was in a matter of days.

Ilka - On Her Knees to Wonderful Freedom

Ilka is a very senior Technical Manager in a global technology company.

I had felt her pain for years. She is an incredibly intelligent lady. She was so proud that people trusted her, that they could rely on her to do a great job. She would never let her customers down. Yet, she was taking an absolute hammering. Deep down, she must have known what I could clearly see. She was on her knees. What is more, though she loved her family, now, she begrudged them the time they wanted from her. She never had time for friends.

Eventually, her immune system became so weak that she was ill all the time. Fortunately, it caused her to reach out for help.

In 2 hours flat, we worked out how she could delegate 20% of her work to her staff. She had always been worried that her colleagues would make mistakes. Yet, once she decided how to help them, they came up to speed quickly. Then, she quickly got well and is her shining self again. She is now performing as her full, brilliant self, and loving her life. She prizes the extra time she has for herself, her family, her friends, and to just be.

QUESTION

Did these stories resonate with you? What similarities can you see with your life? How can you learn from them? How could you set yourself up so you can thrive too?

I have so many more customer stories I could share. With every single one, as soon as they decided that there had to be a better way, we found a great solution. It will be exactly the same with you.

Taking Your First Steps From Stressed to Loving Life

Here are 4 first steps for you:

1. The first and most important step: Decide that you want to feel really alive. That you have had enough of just existing, coping, what the French call "Commute. Work. Sleep."

2. Paint a picture of how, even in your current job and life situation, you would love to work, e.g.

    o What pace/rhythm would feel great?
    o What would you enjoy doing regularly?
    o What space/time for you would you love?
    o What else would each day, each week look like that would set you up to be the best version of yourself?

Take some time with this—the clearer you become, the easier it will be.

3. Ask yourself: If a friend of mine or one of my children were in the situation I am in, and I really wanted to help him or her to break out of it, exactly what would I tell her to do?

4. Every day, breathe in for 4 counts, hold it for 7, and release slowly with a sigh for 8 counts. This is one of many very powerful ways to unwind your nervous system and re-centre yourself. Do it several times each day and you will notice an even greater impact.

If you have found this chapter helpful, the full Stressed 2 Loving Life methodology is designed to do exactly what it says it will.

It:

1. Guides you to define what thriving looks like, to you, with such depth and inspiring clarity that it acts as a magnet, pulling you towards it

2. Clears the blocks that cause you stress

3. Teaches you how to set yourself up to flow with life so you can enjoy each day

4. Describes how to love yourself and to become your own best friend so you always feel deeply valued and supported

5. Shows you how to give yourself what you need to bring out the best in yourself

6. Explains how to get out of your noisy head into your body. So you feel much more, wonderfully, centred and become so much more you, at your very best

Email me at jane@stressed2lovinglife.com, and I will send you a series of gifts to continue your journey:

- The lessons I learnt from burning out
- More great stories of how amazing women cut their stress and started to thrive
- An inspiring picture of what thriving really looks like
- A meditation to calm your nervous system
- The reasons people think they cannot cut their stress or thrive, and why each one is just a misconception

Kerrie D. Stone

Founder of SheThatExists
Minister, Metaphysician, Mystical Life Coach,
Visionary & Creative Director

https://www.linkedin.com/in/rev-kerrie-d-stone-a19964299/
https://www.facebook.com/shethatexists
https://www.instagram.com/shethatexiststheuniteroftribes/
https://shethatexists.com/
https://kerriedstone.com/

Kerrie D. Stone, Founder of SheThatExists, is a former child performer in dance/theater performance arts at Story Book Theater Playhouse in Texas. She is a former gymnast and has performed in parades. A former select corporate softball athlete, she has played several team sports. She is a musician trained in clarinet, piano, and the xylophone, having performed in concert and jazz bands. She is an awarded esthetician. As a former showwoman, she produced her own community show as a single mom. Born a spiritual child, she professed her faith in Creator at age 15. A champion in supporting others in their greatness, she has 36 years of team/leadership experience. Today she is an Ordained Minister in service of life as sacred, a mystical life coach, metaphysician, visionary, polymath, Creative Director, and Comedian. Her favorite passion is being momma. She is earning her Masters degree and is a PhD candidate.

The Art of Learning to Trust and Believe in My Self

By Kerrie D. Stone

The Art of learning to trust and believe in my Self was considered an act of defiance and rebellion in my family of origin. I was never allowed to think for my Self. I was not allowed to express my thoughts or my feelings. My thoughts did not matter. I was not allowed to even express my thoughts or my feelings. My thoughts did not matter. Thoughts and feelings were an act of defiance. When I would try to use my voice, it was not only an act of defiance; it was outright rebellion, and I was punished. Mom and Dad were not loving. They were not parents. Parents are supposed to be able to love, care, and nurture, right?

Using my voice was called "talking back". Using my voice came with severe punishment—the big threat from Mom in her bitter, cold voice, "Wait until your dad gets home". Then, Dad would come home, and I would attempt to tell the truth, and try to stand up for my Self. This only made things worse, voicing my side of the story—the truth of what happened, expressing my Self, using my voice—this only enraged my mom and dad, and of course, we all know what happened from there—the BELT ALWAYS came out.

The Belt, bend over, the Shame. The "This hurts him more than it hurts me."

This was the cycle of abuse in my home. If I opened my mouth, if I spoke, it was defiance. I can remember this from the time I was 11. Memories going back to my earlier years are more scattered. I'm not sure if I want to recover all the memories, if I'm strong enough to recover them. Protecting my Self growing up was an act of defiance. Expressing my voice and my feelings was definitely disobedience.

The more I expressed my truth, the more I was punished for my disobedience and defiance. I was told by my dad that I was lucky. I was lucky that my mom didn't throw me out on the streets when I was 13 years old. All I did was stand up for my Self, using my voice to protect and stand up for my Self and tell the truth, and so I did not understand.

Now that I'm older, I have more awareness and understanding. See, when I started my menstrual cycle at 13, my mom told me, "Well, you are a woman now." That was the education that I received about my menstrual cycle. That is all. The education that I received from my dad was, "If you have sex, I will kill you."

Dad said that two women can't live in the same house together, and so that is why I was lucky that at 13, I did not get thrown out to the streets. I suppose Dad thought he was some sort of savior for keeping me off the streets at 13 years old. At least, now I have an idea of why my mom always treated me so poorly. Mom constantly threatened to throw me out on the streets from 13 years onward—it became a game that she would play on me, I suppose. Mom and my older sister would always gang up on me and call me a brat and mentally and emotionally work together to traumatize me. These are the memories that I have of my family. It was a constant battle of being bullied by my mom and sister and then being threatened by my mom constantly "wait until your dad gets home"—the same patterns of me standing up for my Self, trying to tell the truth, and my dad not being able to listen to me because my mom would threaten to leave my dad. Then, of course, the belt always came out directed at me while my mom would sometimes watch and, other times, turn a blind eye because of her guilt and her shame. Dad always hurt me pretty bad. Mom's typical behavior was to deny her own bad behavior and turn a blind eye to my pain, the shame that dad would try to place into me from his own bad behaviors, and for the most part, my memories of my sister are completely blacked out. Other than her bullying me most of my life, we were never close, even in my desperate attempts of trying to get her to love me and accept me as her friend. She was the big sister and so all I ever wanted was for her to love me and accept me as her friend. At 13, I didn't know this was considered a dysfunctional family; however, I knew something was not right and something was not normal. Athletics, jazz, and concert band kept me pretty busy—that and hanging out with friends. I played the piano, clarinet, and xylophone. Dad put me in private corporate softball. As long as I performed in public as they expected me to, then I thought things could be better at home. The belt always came out, though, the patterns with my parents stayed the same. I was always the target of their dysfunction, and I was the scapegoat for all of their guilt and shame.

Apparently, I had what is called a "strong will". Mom and Dad didn't like that I took up for my Self and that I had a "strong will". They definitely did not like that I had a voice, and my feelings were not recognized at all. Mom and Dad made sure that I performed well in public, having me perform on stage in dance and theater since I was three. I won first place in the "Strut" when I was 4 at Storybook Playhouse Theater. My parents made sure I performed well in public, they even had me performing in parades when I was little. I have made the newspaper several times. However, I was not allowed to have any photos or newspaper clippings of my performances as a child star. Dad put me on a corporate select softball team when I was 12. I helped take my team to Tri-State by hitting the winning home run with someone else on base to help my team win in my state, which got us to Tri-State. I wonder how much my dad made from that since it was a corporate select team. He never told me, and I never received a dime from it.

In 9th grade, when I was 14/15, we moved to a new school in a different state for my dad's job. Things only got worse. Once we moved, I felt like a fish out of water. I wasn't playing sports. Dad said that I wasn't good at sports anymore because I had large breasts. Dad made me feel very uncomfortable about my breasts. Mom never talked to me about my hormones or my menstrual cycle, and there was never a talk about "sex".

I tried to play sports but was insecure because of my dad and his thoughts on my breasts. My parents didn't keep me in music lessons and so that fell away as well. I won in my 9th grade debate team, but that seemed to be it. I was getting bullied at school all the time. I tried karate but was assaulted and strangled outside the karate building by a male teammate. During this time, I was living/staying with my dad's co-worker. I didn't feel safe at home, so when I was given the opportunity to come to live and stay with my dad's co-worker and given a job to get paid to take their kids to school and pick them up for school, I knew it was "God" protecting me and looking after me. When I was assaulted outside of the karate school by a fellow karate mate, I called the people I was living with for help, after all, my parents had never protected me once. I was 16 years old when this happened. My parents have never cared for me, even though I knew that I was on my own, after all, I was "lucky" that I wasn't thrown out on the streets at 13 because of my mom and dad's false belief that "two women could not live in the same home" and I was "grown and a woman" at 13, according to my mom and dad's sick mentally and spiritually unhealthy belief system.

Not only were things bad at home, and karate class became a place of terror, but the school I went to was trying to force the integration of race. I didn't know it was a "thing," and it was a very scary situation. They would bus the "white kids" over to the "black side of town," and they would bus the "black kids" over to the "white side of town". I had no clue what was going on. My parents never explained anything to me. I didn't even know what racism or hatred was. Every day, I went to my Biology class, I was called "Casper", "Ghost" or "whitey" by a classmate. Every day, I was bullied. The teacher we had was in his last year and about to retire. He never stopped the bullying and name-calling and allowed it. After enough ongoing name-calling and bullying and no one intervening or stopping it, one day, I just threw my book at the guy calling me names—I had had it. I told him to stop calling me names, but he would never stop. I hit him on the side of the shoulder with my biology book. I knew better than to aim at his face. I still had my softball throwing arm, and I was going to take it up for my Self—after all, no one else was. I didn't have parents who cared for me or loved me. The guy who bullied me daily told me to come pick up the book. He wanted me to be in fear of him because of his race, because he was a male, and because of his strength. I was walking with the Creator, so I didn't have fear. I went to pick up the book, and he picked me up by my neck, strangled me, and held me in the air in front of the entire classroom. I could have died from being strangled and him impeding my breath. This happened in Texas, and in Texas, it's a third-degree felony. The teacher did nothing to stop this, of course. Once the guy let me down back on the ground, I grabbed my backpack and took off running to the principal's office, completely traumatized. I wasn't protected. We both got the same punishment because of the political race wars, I suppose. My parents didn't explain anything to me, and they didn't protect me. My dad just yelled at me because I "embarrassed him" because he was supposed to come in and speak at my school in my driver's education class on Railroad Safety for a Program Called "Operation Safety," and my dad said he was "embarrassed" because his daughter was suspended from school when he was coming to speak. Once again, they showed no concern for my safety or my well-being, and I was not allowed any form of trauma counseling and was never given any love, hugs, or care.

I later learned that the beatings with the belt were to break my spirit. This is what they do to "defiant" children and teens who have a voice, know the truth, and stand up for themselves. I don't know if this was just for boys and girls or just girls.

At 15 years old, I knew that I obviously did not have conscious parents or a healthy, happy, functioning, loving, caring, warm home or family life. As soon as I received my permit to drive, I got my first job taking my dad's co-worker's kids to school and picking them up. I lived with them and felt safer with them than I did around my parents and sibling. As soon as I felt confident, I got another job as a cashier at a Mexican restaurant called "Crazy Jose's". I spent all my money on books. Self-help books, written by counselors and PhDs. I purchased books on spirituality and religion. I purchased books on health and the dangers of the pharmaceutical industry, and I started studying everything I could about mental health and spirituality. When my dad felt he could not control me, he would threaten me by throwing away all of my books because he knew that I loved reading and learning. They don't want the slaves to learn, you know! 😊 I knew the school system was not teaching me the truth. I started paying attention to the guidance that I was receiving inside from my Intuition and from the Creator within. I had recognized and remembered that Guidance from within as a Child and I returned to that voice within for solace and for learning and continued education. It was during this time I started going to church. I was invited by the local Baptist girl, her dad was the local pastor. It helped, it was better than being at home. It was during this time that I gave my life to God publically in the Baptist church. Shortly after this, my dad beat me again with a belt, and the shame was so bad this time that I went into my closet and prayed to God to die. My dad heard me praying to God to die and came back with a razor, handed it to me, and told me to kill my Self. Of course, my mom turned a blind eye to this as usual the whole entire time, and she always brought my dad to his "anger" because he was forced to beat me or throw me out on the streets. This beating came because a friend and I drove to the next town over to a football game because we were invited by a boy. My car ended up breaking down. We didn't know we did anything wrong. My mom and dad had to drive and come get us and restart my car. Of course, my dad separated me and my friend, and I had to ride with him. He called me every single horrible name in the book, including 'whore' on the way home. After my dad told me to kill my Self that night, something in me was never the same. I can still feel the pain inside today. I begged my mom and dad to take me to counseling over that incident. My dad had a great job in upper management for the railroad, and so they had really good insurance. My parents always had nice things: nice homes and new cars, material possessions. My parents cared more about "keeping up with the Jones" than they did over loving me or teaching me or communicating with me. They didn't teach me about life and all. In fact, they taught me that I am not them and will never be them. They taught me everything that I Am not.

I was very suicidal for some time after my dad handed me the razor and told me to kill my Self. After enough begging, they took me to a counselor one time. The counselor was a female. My parents spent the entire counseling session degrading, disparaging, and shaming me. I remember feeling more suicidal than ever. The counselor knew that my parents were very mentally, emotionally, and spiritually ill. The counselor knew that my parents were not capable of loving and caring for me. I remember that I had about 10 minutes to talk to the counselor. She knew that I was doomed, that I would never be back in her office again, and that the only hope she had was to give me directions to purchase a book to read to help me. I don't remember the counselor's name, I just know that I knew that she knew that this was her only chance to help me, and she would never see me again. The book she referred to me was *Reviving Ophelia: Saving the Selves of Adolescent Girls*, written and authored by Mary Pipher, PhD. She was correct, and I was correct, my parents never let me go back to her as a counselor again. My parents were terrified that they would be seen as the horrible abusers, unloving parents, and severely broken people that they were and still are today. I have teaching and wisdom videos up on my "I Am Simply Kerrie" Facebook page of my teaching and sharing from my life, my life wisdom, and reading from Mary Pipher, PhD, book today.

I purchased the book. I started reading it. I still have it in my master's library collection today. I kept to my Self in school. My nickname in school became "Bible Girl". I stayed mostly to my Self and only spoke to other students in school when they came to me for wisdom, guidance, or care. I was the most spiritually advanced in my family—I still am today. I was invited to a Pentecostal church by some teenagers and their early 20s something in a mall. I started to go to church there at 16. I was baptized in a Pentecostal church. I fell in love with Revival and Teachers who would come and teach at the church in revival meetings. I received what was called the "Holy Spirit" at the church. My parents even came to church and got baptized, as well as my sister and my grandpa. It was a one-time thing for them. My dad played golf with the pastor of the church a couple of times, and they ended up selling my second cousin, who was living with us, to an orphanage. I knew that was wrong. I was just 16 years old at the time and didn't know exactly what was going on. I tried to play sports in high school, but it just didn't work out. I stayed with God and just read my Bible. My relationship with my Maker has always been my saving grace and going within. I had one or two friends from church and that's about it. I really fell in love with God and the revivals that I attended. I was exploited by older guys at my cashier restaurant job when I was 16 or 17, my parents never protected me. For the most part, I think I blocked out most of my teen years to survive. After graduation, I was "on my own"—my parents moved out of state, and my sister lived in another state with her husband, who was in the Marine Corps. My first job out of high school was for the United States Post Office. I passed a test and got a job doing data entry. It didn't last long because a guy friend I had made was stalking me, broke into my apartment one time when I was not there, left the door unlocked, and turned the heat up in my apartment as high as it would go. He was psychotic. I even had a police officer who would often follow me home, stalking me, showing up at my apartment, and knocking on the door. I remember just hiding in the bathroom crying, playing my favorite female worship singer at the time, Kathy Troccoli, and praying for God to protect me and save me. There was no point in telling my parents, I knew they would not protect me. I was "on my own," as my dad said, and I remembered how lucky I was that I didn't get thrown out on the streets at 13 like my mom wanted to do to me. I remembered to be thankful to my dad for not killing me and for not throwing me out on the streets like my mom wanted him to.

This is just a sample sharing of what I have overcome. I suppose I have defied the odds, and most of all, somehow, I did not allow my Self to become just a statistic. Normally, I would not share any of this, because it was buried in the deep recesses of my memories, and possibly it's too taboo to share with society. I felt called to share this for such a time as this because we can defy the odds. We can overcome. We can create the impossible with our lives. We can do anything that we set our minds and hearts to. We can trust the Creator and the good in life with our lives. We can do the impossible and we can overcome everything with faith in the goodness of our Maker and trust and belief in our Self. The whole time I was going to church, I never had one pastor tell me to believe in my Self. I learned that a male pastor was never going to elevate me. The first individual who told me to believe in my Self was my University President, who was a female Ordained Minister. She helped me to realize that I can trust and believe in my Self because the Creator is within me (that I Am never alone), and I Am not separate as a female from the Creator within me. She let me know that believing in my Self is a rite of passage. I now believe in my Self more than ever and see my parents for the broken souls that they are. I've learned forgiveness and how to love people who are not safe for me safely from a distance.

I encourage you to believe in your Self and who you are. I also want you to know it is safe to not only trust your Self, to believe in your Self, but it is also safe for you to live in your heart and feel everything inside you and be fully alive. I believe in you. The Creator believes in you. You are safe to believe in yourself. It is safe to trust your Self and listen to your inner voice—the voice of truth—your soul talking to you and guiding you from within, the Creator within.

You see, We get this hand of cards we are dealt with in life—we all do. Whether it's "good or bad", the whole point is that we can overcome and defy the odds—we can love with a whole heart, and we can overcome anything in our life. Our Spirit is unbreakable. When we live in our hearts, we are indestructible. No one can steal our light and our goodness from us. This is what I want the reader to get from the sharing of my heart and soul. No one can steal our light, and no one can steal our goodness. Our light and goodness belong to us. Our true essence is the soul, and no one can take that from us. We can reclaim everything that was supposedly stolen from us because we are the rightful owners of us at all times. The Creator has wonderful plans for our lives and we are born for not just goodness but greatness. I hope the sharing of my truth has been inspiring to you and of great encouragement.

There is a saying that the two greatest days of your life are the day you were born, and the other greatest day is the day you find out the purpose of why you were born. If I can be of any support to you in your journey or life, please let me know. I am born to support others in their greatness and in their soul's purpose. This is part of my purpose in life, and it's an honor to be able to share part of my soul's journey with you. I am a Destiny Guide and am here to help elevate others because we are all born with great purpose. Hold onto your heart and soul, for you are your heart and you are your soul—don't let go, for this life is a glorious creation, and we are born for greatness.

In Honor of All of Life as Sacred,
Reverend Kerrie D. Stone

Kimberly Laverdure

Kimberly Laverdure, The Virtual Life Alchemist
Business Coach & Consutant

https://www.linkedin.com/in/kimberly-laverdure-the-virtual-life-alchemist-b23745a8/
https://www.facebook.com/kimberly.smith72/
https://www.instagram.com/kimberly_laverdure/
https://virtuallifealchemist.com
https://yourneighborhoodwitch.com

Kimberly Laverdure is a sought-after Business Coach, Consultant, and Virtual Life Alchemist with over 15 years of experience helping entrepreneurs streamline their operations and reclaim their time. Through her signature Systemize for Success™ framework, Kimberly empowers soul-driven entrepreneurs to leverage technology and automation to scale their businesses while maintaining balance and joy.

As the founder of Systemize for Success™, she has guided business owners, coaches, healers, and service providers to align their businesses with their intuition and vision. Her holistic approach turns overwhelm into clarity and chaos into flow, helping clients achieve both freedom and success.

Kimberly's passion is simplifying complex processes so entrepreneurs can build sustainable businesses, work smarter, and avoid burnout—all while infusing fun and play into their journey.

Defying the Darkness: A Journey from Despair to Empowerment

By Kimberly Laverdure

Standing on the edge of a vast, turbulent ocean, I could feel the icy spray cut through my skin, as if the bitter cold wanted to crawl inside me. The waves crashed violently against jagged cliffs, threatening to pull me into the abyss below—a place darker and deeper than I ever imagined. The wind screamed in my ears, drowning out my thoughts, matching the chaos that roared within me.

This was my life: a relentless storm of emotional violence and despair battering me from all sides, leaving me to question if I had the strength to stand, or if I'd finally be swallowed whole.

Have you ever been there? Have you ever felt like no matter how hard you fought, the darkness would consume you? Perhaps you feel it now.

My story isn't just a recounting of events; it's a raw journey through pain, resilience, and transformation. It's about finding light in the darkest places and discovering an indomitable strength within.

The Awakening

On October 17, 2006, the morning after my 13th wedding anniversary, I stared blankly at the ceiling. Sixteen years of severe emotional and verbal abuse had hollowed me out. My husband's relentless cycle of degradation—"You're such a stupid bitch! Can't you do anything right?"—followed by manipulative love bombing had eroded my spirit to the point where I felt like a mere shadow of myself.

That morning, a numbness settled over me—a protective shield against the pain that had become my constant companion. The recent loss of my beloved grandparents, who had been pillars of unconditional love in my life, underscored life's brevity and fragility. Their passing was a stark reminder that time waits for no one. As tears welled up, a quiet resolve formed within me: I couldn't spend another moment in a marriage that was slowly killing me.

I had recently found a job I loved, working as a Kitchen Designer. It was a modest position, but it began restoring my confidence and sense of self-worth. For the first time in years, I was recognized for my skills and dedication. My colleagues were fun to work with; supervisors valued my work ethic, natural customer service, and leadership abilities. Each day at work was a respite from the turmoil at home.

Summoning every ounce of courage, I decided it was time to reclaim my life. Telling him was one of the hardest things I've ever done. My heart pounded so loudly I feared it would burst from my chest. As I uttered the words, "I don't love you anymore," his eyes flashed with a mixture of disbelief and hurt.

His reaction was immediate and intense. He oscillated between pleading for another chance—promising he'd change, that things would be different—and having our children write me letters begging me not to break up the family. His mother called me, screaming accusations over the phone. "How could you do this after 16 years, you bitch!" The weight of their condemnation pressed heavily upon me, but I held firm.

He moved into his parents' house to give me space to think. Then the stalking began. Late at night, I'd catch a glimpse of his car lurking at the end of the street, headlights extinguished but engine ominously humming—a constant reminder that escape was an illusion. The shadows seemed to stretch and twist under the dim streetlights, amplifying my fear.

A shiver would course through me as I felt the weight of his gaze piercing through the walls, eroding the sanctuary of my home. Every ring of the phone sent a jolt through my body; his voice on the other end, cold and insistent, demanding to know who I was with, what I was doing, and why I dared to seek solace in the company of friends. The boundaries of my freedom shrank with each passing day, suffocated by his relentless presence.

He finally told me he wasn't staying with his parents anymore and moved back in, against all our "agreements." The violation of this boundary was the final straw. I realized that my safety—and that of my children—was at greater risk than ever before.

The Battle for My Children

When I finally moved out with our three boys, ages 7, 9, and 11, I felt a profound sense of freedom—a lightness I hadn't experienced in years. The new house was small but cozy, decorated with my things and feeling like my own place for the first time in my adult life.

But the relief was short-lived. I had lied to get away from him, telling him we would work on our marriage but that I needed space. When he finally realized I was saying it in words only, he weaponized our children against me, telling them, "Your mother doesn't want to be a family anymore. She chose to leave us." The subtle brainwashing had begun, and I saw the confusion and hurt in their innocent eyes.

The stalking continued; on social media, he monitored my every move. He drove past my house, making notes of cars in the driveway, questioning when they were there and who they belonged to. He approached my colleagues, fishing for information, and enlisted friends on social media to spy on me. All of it he tried to use against me in court, twisting innocent interactions into fabricated evidence.

What followed was a five-year legal nightmare. He vowed, "You're leaving me? Then, you're no longer fit to be a mother. I will do everything in my power to keep my children from you." And he did.

Court summons became a regular part of my life. Each appearance was a harrowing ordeal, with his attorney painting me as unstable and unfit.

The judge, a stern man with a cold gaze, seemed predisposed against me. During one hearing, he glanced over the paperwork and, without allowing me to speak, ruled in favor of my ex-husband. "Custody will be granted to the father. Visitation rights to the mother every other weekend." His gavel struck like a thunderclap, sealing my fate.

I was shattered. Every day was a struggle to hold onto hope. Nights were the hardest—spent curled up in the bathtub, hot water turning cold as I wept uncontrollably. The silence of the house echoed the emptiness I felt inside. The pain of being alienated from my children was unbearable. Questions tormented me: How could the system fail us so profoundly? What more could I have done?

Amidst this darkness, a kind man we'll call Michael entered my life. We met at a local bar, introduced by a mutual friend on a night we were out celebrating our birthdays. I had never believed in love at first sight before this, but as we said hi to each other and locked eyes, there was no one else in the music-filled, crowded bar. His gentle demeanor and genuine interest in my well-being were a balm to my wounded soul.

Michael's support was a lifeline, helping me rediscover myself beyond the roles of wife and mother. For three years, he stood by me as I navigated the turbulent waters of loss and identity. He reminded me of the joy in simple things—a walk in the park, the taste of a well-made meal, the warmth of a heartfelt conversation. Through his unwavering kindness, I began to see a glimmer of the strong woman I once was.

Ultimately, I made the excruciating decision to stop fighting. The legal system had failed me repeatedly, and continuing the battle was destroying what little was left of me. Letting go of the daily struggle was the hardest thing I've ever done, but it was necessary for my survival and for any hope of future reconciliation.

Rebuilding and Rediscovering

Physically, I was also falling apart. A ruptured disc led to multiple back surgeries, leaving me permanently disabled. The searing pain was a constant reminder of my fragility. Diagnosed with fibromyalgia, IBS, anxiety, depression, and PTSD, I felt like my body was betraying me at every turn. Simple tasks became monumental challenges. Unable to work, I questioned, "Who am I, if not a mother or a contributing member of society?"

Then, a beacon of hope appeared. My sister-in-law, Sarah, told me they had just lost their Editor-in-Chief. I knew I could not only do the job but do it even better. So, I told them exactly why they should hire me. The magazine focused on women's empowerment—a cause that resonated deeply with me. Immersed in a community of inspiring women, I began to understand the power of shared stories and collective resilience. I had to prove myself, and I embraced the challenge wholeheartedly.

Diving into the role reignited my confidence and reminded me of my capabilities. I immersed myself in writing, editing, and curating stories that inspired others. Exchanging my services for coaching, I began deep inner healing work. Through therapy and mentorship, I confronted the traumas of my past, learning to forgive myself and release the burdens I had carried for so long.

I remarried and had two more beautiful children—a spirited son and a radiant daughter who brought immeasurable joy into my life. For a while, life seemed to offer a second chance at happiness. Our home was filled with laughter, bedtime stories, and the pitter-patter of little feet.

But soon, cracks appeared. My second husband, whom we'll call David, began to resent the responsibilities of family life. His once affectionate demeanor turned distant. He started staying out late, his occasional drinks escalating into a nightly ritual. The smell of alcohol clung to him like a toxic cloud.

One evening, after tucking the kids into bed, I tried to talk to him about our growing distance. "David, I'm worried about you... about us," I began hesitantly. He scoffed, avoiding my gaze. "You're overreacting, you're just so sensitive," he replied curtly. The dismissal stung, and a familiar feeling of isolation crept in.

Taking a Stand

His struggles with alcoholism worsened after the tragic loss of his parents—his mother to cancer and his father soon after. Grief consumed him, and his anger became unbearable. He mistreated our children, snapping at them for minor annoyances, his patience worn thin.

We moved to Florida, hoping a change of scenery might help. For a brief period, the Sunshine State seemed to lift his spirits. But the reprieve was fleeting. His drinking escalated, and his abusive behavior intensified.

On Christmas Eve, he returned home intoxicated and enraged, gifts forgotten. He had missed the traditional activities, and the kids were already asleep. Fear tightened its grip on me. That night, I realized I was in another abusive relationship. The cycle was repeating, and I needed to break it—not just for me, but for my children.

I focused on expanding my virtual assistant business, determined to secure financial independence. Late nights were spent planning and holding live events, managing client projects, and learning new skills. His anger peaked when he destroyed my phone in a fit of rage, the shattered screen mirroring the fractured state of our marriage.

Fearful for our safety, I packed up the children and spent the summer at my family's cabin—a place of refuge nestled among towering trees and a serene bay. There, I found solace in nature's embrace, contemplating our future. I asked myself, "What kind of life do I want for my children? What legacy am I leaving them?"

Upon returning, nothing had changed. David's destructive patterns continued. One night, he invaded my personal space, bursting into my bedroom uninvited. The violation was the final straw. I set firm boundaries—moving his belongings to a separate room and installing locks on my bedroom door.

His retaliation was swift and violent. He broke down doors, his face contorted with rage, screaming and intimidating me in front of our terrified children. The look of fear in their eyes ignited a fierce protective instinct within me. I knew I had to act.

I sought help from SafeSpace, a domestic abuse nonprofit. Walking into their office, I felt a mix of shame and relief. Admitting I needed help was daunting, but their compassionate support made all the difference. With their guidance, I obtained a restraining order. For the first time, the legal system protected me. The judge believed me; my lawyer advocated for me. Standing in that courtroom, I felt a surge of empowerment. I was no longer voiceless.

Embracing Empowerment

With my abuser removed from our lives, I poured my energy into personal growth and my business. My virtual assistant work flourished, evolving into roles as an Online Business Manager and Operations Director. I took courses, attended seminars, and networked with industry leaders. Each achievement was a testament to my resilience.

Now, as an Operations Specialist and Business Consultant, I h others streamline their operations and reclaim their passion. Guiding clients to overcome their own obstacles brings me profound fulfillment. I see pieces of my journey reflected in theirs, and together, we forge paths to success.

Today, I am married to a supportive husband who is a wonderful stepdad and champions my growth and business endeavors. His unwavering belief in me has been a cornerstone of my continued healing and success.

My health remained a challenge. Chronic pain from degenerative disc disease and fibromyalgia persisted. At 51, a diagnosis of Hashimoto's disease finally explained years of fatigue and weight gain. Initially, the diagnosis felt overwhelming—a new mountain to climb. But I chose resilience over resignation.

I educated myself about the disease, devouring books and articles. I adapted my diet, embracing anti-inflammatory foods and eliminating gluten and processed sugars. Gentle exercises like yoga and daily walks became essential, nurturing both body and mind. I practiced mindfulness and meditation, learning to listen to my body's needs. Managing Hashimoto's became part of my journey, teaching me to nurture myself with compassion and patience.

Reconnecting and Healing

Reconnecting with my children became a central focus. My second oldest son reached out unexpectedly at his high school graduation. "Mom, can we talk?" he said to me. My heart raced as we walked to a secluded spot in the parking lot. "The past is the past, and I don't want to live there anymore. I want us to be a part of each other's lives." My grin felt like it would split my face, and we hugged for the first time in years.

My youngest son and I maintained a close bond throughout the years. We cherished our time together—finding sea glass on the shores of the lake, playing video games, and sharing overnights. Even with his blessing for me to move to Florida, we stayed in touch. His unwavering love was a constant source of strength.

This past summer brought a profound blessing: my oldest son came back into my life, along with his wife and children. He told my parents they were coming up to the family camp. I asked if he knew I would be there, and they said yes. "It's been a long time coming, but he's ready," they told me. My oldest granddaughter had asked where I was and why she couldn't spend time with me.

Our reunion was filled with tentative smiles and light-hearted conversations. I got to play with my grandchildren, getting to know them and talking with my son and daughter-in-law. Being called "Grandma" couldn't have been better. My heart swelled with a joy I hadn't felt in years, a sense of completeness washing over me.

Through therapy and self-reflection, I learned to forgive myself for the guilt I carried. I released the weight of past regrets, understanding that I did the best I could with the circumstances I faced. I embraced the present, finding joy in the laughter of my grandchildren, the warmth of family gatherings, and the simple pleasures of everyday life.

Co-parenting with my ex-husband remains challenging; he is civil only when it suits him. By setting firm boundaries and choosing not to engage, I am learning to keep my own peace.

A Message of Hope

My journey has been one of immense struggle but also profound growth. I've learned that setting boundaries is an act of self-love, that my voice matters, and that I am responsible for my own happiness. I've transitioned from being a victim to a survivor, and now, a thriver.

To anyone feeling overwhelmed by life's relentless waves, know that you are not alone. The darkness may seem endless, but within you lies a reservoir of strength waiting to be tapped. It's okay to feel lost—it's a natural part of the journey—but don't stay there. Reach out and take that first step, no matter how small. Seek support, believe in yourself, and keep moving forward.

There were moments when I questioned everything, when despair threatened to consume me. But each time, I chose to rise. I chose to believe that I was worthy of love, respect, and happiness. And so are you.

Remember, every setback is a setup for a comeback. Your journey is unique, and your strength is unparalleled.

As I continue on my path, I carry with me the lessons of my past but no longer let them define me. I'm grateful for the resilience I've discovered and the life I've built. I stand here today not as someone who has all the answers, but as someone who has walked through the fire and emerged stronger.

I breathe deeply, honoring who I have become and who I am becoming. Placing my hand over my heart, I whisper, "I love you." It's a daily affirmation—a reminder of the journey I've undertaken and the self-love I've cultivated.

Epilogue

My hope is that my story touches you deeply, that you realize you are not alone. May it serve as a beacon of resilience, guiding you through your own journey with courage and determination. Remember, as Rumi wisely said, "*The wound is where the light enters.*" Embrace your scars; they are a testament to your strength.

About the Author

Kimberly Laverdure is a successful businesswoman, Operations Specialist and Business Consultant, mother of five, and grandmother of five—with another on the way. She has transformed her personal trials into a source of strength and inspiration for others. Through her work and her story, she aims to empower individuals to overcome adversity and embrace their own resilience.

Learn more at https://virtuallifealchemist.com

Michele Benevento

Chakra Belly Dance

https://www.linkedin.com/in/michele-benevento-a1490323/
https://www.facebook.com/profile.php?id=61568266462547
https://www.instagram.com/micheledbenevento/
https://www.skool.com/chakra-bellydance-4215/about

Michele Benevento is the creator of Chakra Belly Dance a program designed to take you into your dark feminine energy, dance with the darkness, ground into the sensual and ignite your Divine Feminine fire! An innovative, sensual, healing journey created based on her background and training in psychology, Reiki, sound healing, NLP, spiritual coaching and belly dance.

After life altering events, Michele recognized how societal conditioning disconnected her from her dark feminine energy influencing her decisions that led her to a life now shattered and no clear direction to follow. Dark feminine energy embraces that which society deems taboo. Through such conditioning and traumatic experiences, we learn to disassociate from our authentic selves, ultimately diminishing our ability to create the lives and experiences we desire for fear of defying the norm set before us. But now, She Defies and she invites you to join her in that defiance!

Dance With Your Demons

By Michele Benevento

"Be still, and know that I am God. You will fall but you will fly."

These are the words I heard the Holy Spirit say to me on the first day when my husband had taken his girlfriend on vacation for her birthday. I knew he had been cheating but could not prove it and of course when I confronted him a couple of months prior, he staunchly denied it, initiated a fight, accused me of being crazy and stormed out of the house stating he would be staying at a hotel because he wasn't going to stay another moment dealing with my insanity, as he grabbed some towels and clothes and walked out the door. I recall at that moment thinking to myself, "Towels, hmmm, an odd thing to bring with you when you are going to a hotel, especially since I knew that he had never brought towels with him before when he had stayed at a hotel." But, I digress, back to the Las Vegas trip with the girlfriend.

In the weeks leading up to this trip, I knew his story of going away with his best friend was complete bullshit! But what could I do, once again, I could not prove it, while every fiber of my being was screaming, "LIES, ALL LIES!!!" Yet, I still played the dutiful wife, "Of course, honey, you deserve a break, you work hard." Meanwhile, in my mind, I am screaming, "You go out all the time, and away on business trips that I know are not all business! All the while, I am home, caring for our three young children. I am always here alone caring for them!" I was angry but as history had proven any expression of anger on my part was met with an offensive attack leading to a stressful environment that I did not wish to inflict upon my children, or myself. Once again, I betrayed myself and I remained silent. The night before his trip he even had the audacity to expect me to pack for him! I am embarrassed to admit, I did it, once again out of dread of the consequences and fear of the disruption of peace.

Peace, that's comical, what peace? The realization that my life had become a series of managing the tyrannical tantrums and outbursts of a volatile personality was evident in my reflection. For months prior to this trip, I gazed into the mirror only to behold a face devoid of color, vibrancy and emotion. When did I become an empty shell of a person? When did I lose me... my hopes, my dreams...my spirit? The realization was staggering, overwhelming and devastating. Everyday, I would look into the mirror knowing I was on the verge of an emotional, mental and physical collapse. I could not take much more and I contemplated placing myself in the hospital, just to have a break! Every time that thought entered my mind, I heard God tell me "NO! You can do this, hold on!" I had this claircognizance that it was all going to be ending soon and that if I had made that choice there may be dire consequences, possibly that break being used against me to take my children from me. I was at my wit's end with my unhappy marriage completely falling apart, the undeniable betrayal of my husband, my mother dying of ovarian cancer, the possibility of losing my children too was unfathomable. I had to dig deep and find the fortitude to go on.

I was wrestling with so many demons. How did I get here? How did I lose myself? Where did I go so horribly wrong? Can I be the woman I was before this all happened? Do I even want to be the woman I was? After all, it was her choices that led me to this abyss of darkness and torment. But these questions would have to wait.

My mind was racing with thoughts of survival of me and my children, how would I survive financially, I have been a stay at home wife and mother for nearly ten years at this point, how would I provide for myself and my children. Despite everything, I loved this man, he is the father of my children. How could I do this alone? How could I even sleep in that bed alone? This was not the life I had envisioned, this was not the dream. The dream I had since childhood. The beautiful home with white picket fence, adoring husband, beautiful children that we watch grow up and have families of their own. My mind was racing with the thoughts of the past, all the insults, disrespect, neglect, the present reality that I didn't even know the extent of and the future that would never come to pass. Every thought a blade shredding my mind, the poison that gushed from those wounds tearing up my stomach leaving me nauseous, bare, broken and bleeding.

I felt the knife of another betrayal, one that was so long ago, one I had thought I had healed, however, the state of my life currently was a direct reflection of the neglect, abandonment and indifference that I had suffered at the hands of my father. How could this be?!? My mind was reeling, one question reverberated through my brain, "How could this be happening to me?" I have a degree in psychology, I've gone to therapy, I watched my mother go through this and swore it would never happen to me. And, yet, here I was staring down, what felt like the barrel of a gun, that same gun of betrayal pointed directly at my face. With my only option being to pray he didn't pull the trigger.

BANG! The bullet of DISRESPECT!.
BANG! The bullet of BETRAYAL!
BANG! The bullet of ABANDONMENT!

The shots just kept coming. The first one knocked me to my knees, the second I was on all fours by the time the fourth and fifth, I was prostrate on the floor. There I was broken and bleeding. My soul was screaming to be set free, every breath was a struggle, at that moment, I turned to God. I found solace and hope in His Word. I had nowhere else to turn, I didn't want to burden my mother, she was in the fight of her life, and it did not look good at all. How could I turn to her with this?

I decided to keep it a secret.I would confront him when he returned from his trip and I would let him know that I knew everything. At this point, I did, the more I turned to God, the more spirit guided me and whispered in my ear the truth of what had been going on but my mortal self was terrified.God had assured me that I would fly but I didn't trust it and I still was clinging tightly to that dream of the white picket fence, husband and children, I had to find a way to make that happen.

I devised a plan, I was sure it would work. I decided to tell him he could have his mistress because I knew deep down he loved me and our family and he would be back. I offered this with conditions, he would not stay out all night, the children were not to know, and once it was done he would be fully present here with me and go to therapy with me to work on the relationship. It could not fail, the idea was to take away the excitement of an affair by allowing it and turn her into the "nagging wife" because I knew she was a young girl that was looking for a husband to start a family of her own, she wanted him to herself. Yes, I decided this is what I would do once he returned from his trip.

When he returned that was precisely what I did. At first it appeared to be working but then he started staying out all night, he wasn't going to be told what he could and could not do. Truth be told, it was the best thing for me. Once he left the house, I started to look younger and less stressed, I started to come alive again. In fact other moms at my children's school started coming up to me and telling me how amazing I looked - I was losing weight, my skin started to glow and my whole face looked lighter, younger. How was this possible while I was going through one of the absolute worst times of my life! I couldn't eat and as exhausted as I was, I was barely sleeping. It was as if my life force was returning.

I wish I could say that this time in my life was the worst of it, but it wasn't. As the separation continued and we marched our way towards divorce, things only got worse for me. My house went into forbearance, my mom's body was failing after all the chemo treatments and perhaps potentially the worst of all was I started to bleed profusely, the way my mother did before she was given her ovarian cancer diagnosis. I went to the doctor and was told I had polyps on my uterus and they would need to do a biopsy to find out if it was malignant. Shortly after this diagnosis, my husband allowed the insurance to lapse ,as he did not want to, or perhaps could not afford, to pay the COBRA benefits, either way it left me without insurance and unable to follow up with what was happening to me.

One night, as I studied the ceiling of my bedroom, a nightly ritual since the devastation of my life as I knew it, I began to think about what my boys' lives would be like without me in it. How would they fare being raised by some random woman they did not know and I was sure looked at them as a necessary evil she had to endure. The thought was like a knife through my heart, and yet the thought of my demise as an escape route from my life, I hate to admit, was a little enticing. I was overwhelmed, I had way more questions than I did answers and was feeling hopeless. At that moment, once again, I turned it over to God. As I lay there administering reiki to myself, I prayed, if you could call it that, it was more like negotiating, somehow in this menagerie I thought I had the upper hand. I said, "Ok, God, here are your options, either kill me quick or heal me, because I cannot and will not do traditional medicine to heal me." Which without insurance wasn't an option anyway. After that night, I continued to perform reiki on myself and pray to God to guide me through it all.

The hits just kept on coming. Three months later my mother, my rock and the only person I had always been able to rely on, went into hospice. I remember the day she made the decision. She was in the hospital because she had a mini stroke and then had another mini stroke while in the hospital. The day she made the decision, my siblings and I were with her at the hospital. She asked my siblings to leave the room so she could speak to me alone. I will never forget what she said to me with tears in her eyes my mother said to me, "I'm sorry, baby, I know you need me now more than ever and I've been fighting all this time to be here for you but I'm so tired now and I just can't fight anymore." Now, what I wanted to say was No Mommy, please don't leave me, I can't do this alone! But I did not, what I said was, "It's ok Mommy, I understand, I know you're tired, I will be alright, I can do this alone." Not one ounce of me believed that at the time but I could see the desperation in my mother's face, I knew she needed me to say I would be ok so she could be at peace. And so, out of love, I said something I did not at all believe.

The truth was I was not alone. I had God, my boys, my siblings and some very good friends. Once again I leaned into prayer and meditation and truthfully, when my mother died, a part of me died and in the days following her death I seemed to adopt an I don't give a fuck attitude. So in the time after my mother's memorial, my husband was angry because he was not allowed to come, it was a dying wish of my mother's that she had my brothers swear to uphold. She did not want him coming back into my life because she knew he was toxic for me. This enraged him and caused him to make threats about you won't get a dime or take my children away from me whatever really would make me upset. The irony is, it backfired and I just stood there and smiled at him which enraged him further. What he failed to understand in that moment was that I did not give a fuck about anything any more, I was numb and there is a certain freedom when you have allowed yourself to feel so much for so long that you are now burnt out on emotion. Logic and intellect take over and you see the truth. You begin to see clearly. It was as if I had suddenly unlocked the matrix.

The truth was even though my ex-husband appeared to be the villain here, he is just as much a wounded character as I. His pathology was one that paraded his demons about allowing them to openly rule his life in order to protect him from being wounded again as he had been in his childhood. My demons were lurking in the shadows, shrouded in shame. I would never allow myself to assert myself so selfishly or demand anything of anyone, that would be a terrifying proposition. The possibility of someone withdrawing their love because I had asserted a boundary was unthinkable to me. My childhood had conditioned me to think I was not deserving, that I had to be "perfect", to believe I had to look perfect, behave perfect, excel in everything, and so I attracted someone that would hold those impossible standards for me to live up to and then constantly move the goalposts! The more I excelled at meeting his expectations, the worse he felt about himself and therefore moved the bar. The more he moved the bar, the more I felt him slipping away and that fear of abandonment and shame would take over. Our demons were in a battle and our true selves oblivious to the whole affair.

I began to recognize the energy imbalances in my chakras that led to my vibrating at a frequency that attracted other wounded, unhealed partners. Until I was willing to bring my demons out of the shadows, look them in the face, call them by name and invite them to be my dance partners in life they would forever be working surreptitiously for a spot on my dance card. They craved attention, respect and love. They were the pieces of me that I thought were unacceptable, shameful and unlovable, so like Cinderella's wicked stepmother had done to her, I locked them in a tower and forbid them to go to the ball. However, in locking them away, I locked away my true self and any hope of healing the traumas I had suffered. It is not the bad things that happen to us that cause trauma as much as how we process them or in most instances, not process them or maladaptively process them that cause the trauma.

When healing the trauma is not deliberately addressed our psyche will then seek out a forum to relive the trauma and work out our maladaptive responses. The traumas we recreate are meant to be pattern interrupts, but without proper guidance and practices the more we traumatize ourselves. The longer and more often we recreate these events in an attempt to heal but don't get to the root and address them properly, the further we push them into the cells of the body thus creating autoimmune disorders. An autoimmune disorder is a condition that results from an anomalous response of the adaptive immune system, wherein it mistakenly targets and attacks healthy functioning parts of the body as if they were foreign organisms.

In essence the longer you persist in a psychological state that betrays your true self the more maladaptive the body becomes and the trauma gets stuck at a cellular level wreaking havoc on the physical body. Our mind has processed the events as our fault and now begins running a program that reflects the punishment we think we deserve. Everything in this world is created twice, once in thought or energetic level and second in the physical or three dimensional world.

This is what led me to create my coaching program and specifically chakra bellydance. It was through education and understanding what I had been through, breathwork to calm the body, meditation and physical expression that I began to embrace the Divine Feminine, including the dark feminine aspects. What are the dark feminine aspects you ask? It is the dynamic of the feminine that defies, the confident woman, that won't be quiet and be the "good girl" when her boundaries have been crossed. It is the feminine that embraces the dark, knowing that it is in the depths of the darkness that her light shines the brightest.

JOIN THE MOVEMENT!
#BAUW

Becoming An Unstoppable Woman With She Rises Studios

She Rises Studios was founded by Hanna Olivas and Adriana Luna Carlos, the mother-daughter duo, in mid-2020 as they saw a need to help empower women worldwide. They are the podcast hosts of the *She Rises Studios Podcast* and Amazon best-selling authors and motivational speakers who travel the world. Hanna and Adriana are the movement creators of #BAUW - Becoming An Unstoppable Woman: The movement has been created to universally impact women of all ages, at whatever stage of life, to overcome insecurities, and adversities, and develop an unstoppable mindset. She Rises Studios educates, celebrates, and empowers women globally.

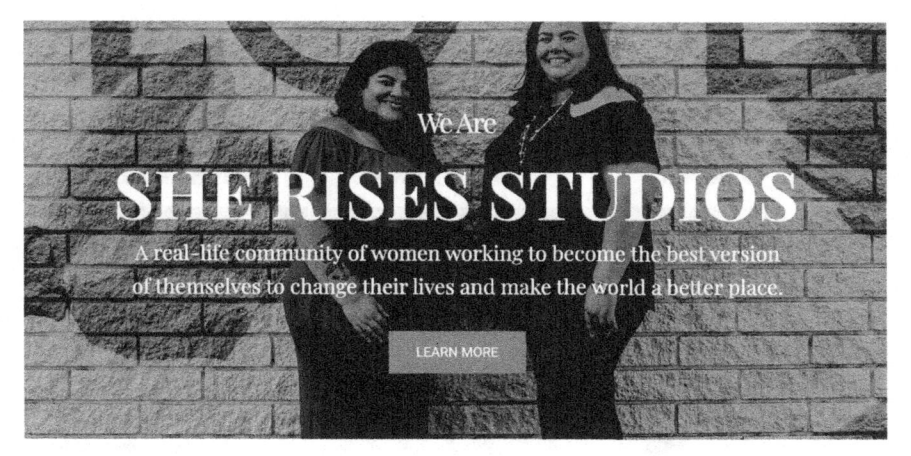

We Are
SHE RISES STUDIOS
A real-life community of women working to become the best version of themselves to change their lives and make the world a better place.

LEARN MORE

Looking to Join Us in our Next Anthology or Publish YOUR Own?

She Rises Studios Publishing offers full-service publishing, marketing, book tour, and campaign services. For more information, contact info@sherisesstudios.com

We are always looking for women who want to share their stories and expertise and feature their businesses on our podcasts, in our books, and in our magazines.

SEE WHAT WE DO

OUR PODCAST

OUR BOOKS

OUR SERVICES

Be featured in the Becoming An Unstoppable Woman magazine, published in 13 countries and sold in all major retailers. Get the visibility you need to LEVEL UP in your business!

Have your own TV show streamed across major platforms like Roku TV, Amazon Fire Stick, Apple TV and more!

Learn to leverage your expertise. Build your online presence and grow your audience with FENIX TV.

https://fenixtv.sherisesstudios.com/

She Defies | 231

Visit www.SheRisesStudios.com to see how YOU can join the #BAUW movement and help your community to achieve the UNSTOPPABLE mindset.

Have you checked out the *She Rises Studios Podcast?*

Find us on all MAJOR platforms: Spotify, IHeartRadio, Apple Podcasts, Google Podcasts, etc.

Looking to become a sponsor or build a partnership?

Email us at info@sherisesstudios.com

SHE RISES
STUDIOS

Made in the USA
Las Vegas, NV
06 February 2025